Secular Philosophy and the Religious Temperament

By the Same Author

Secular Philosophy and the Religious Temperament

Essays 2002–2008

THOMAS NAGEL

OXFORD

UNIVERSITY PRESS

2010

OXFORD
UNIVERSITY PRESS

Oxford University Press, Inc., publishes works that further
Oxford University's objective of excellence
in research, scholarship, and education.

Oxford   New York
Auckland   Cape Town   Dar es Salaam   Hong Kong   Karachi
Kuala Lumpur   Madrid   Melbourne   Mexico City   Nairobi
New Delhi   Shanghai   Taipei   Toronto

With offices in
Argentina   Austria   Brazil   Chile   Czech Republic   France   Greece
Guatemala   Hungary   Italy   Japan   Poland   Portugal   Singapore
South Korea   Switzerland   Thailand   Turkey   Ukraine   Vietnam

Copyright © 2010 Oxford University Press, Inc.

Published by Oxford University Press, Inc.
198 Madison Avenue, New York, New York 10016

www.oup.com

Oxford is a registered trademark of Oxford University Press.

Library of Congress Cataloging-in-Publication Data
Nagel, Thomas, 1937–
Secular philosophy and the religious temperament : essays 2002–2008 / Thomas Nagel.
p.   cm.
Includes bibliographical references and index.
ISBN 978-0-19-539411-5
1. Philosophy.   2. Religion.   3. Justice.   I. Title.
B945.N333S43 2009
191—dc22   2009010609

9 8 7 6 5 4 3 2 1

Printed in the United States of America
on acid-free paper

Preface

Over the past few years, I have been occupied mainly with thoughts about the relation between science and religion, and also secondarily with the interpretation of liberal conceptions of justice and their application to the world as a whole. The first two sections of this collection of essays and reviews correspond roughly to those interests. The third section contains reflections on four admired philosophers, all with a pronounced absorption in the human world. I have revised all the essays slightly.

The material in the first section is preliminary. I hope to pursue the topic, and its larger philosophical implications, more systematically in the future. I am resistant to the broad acceptance of scientific naturalism as a comprehensive world view. Theism is one form that such resistance can take, but I believe that there must be secular alternatives.

—New York, February, 2009

Acknowledgments

The first essay has not been published before. Earlier versions of the other essays appeared in the following places:

2. *The New Republic*, October 23, 2006.

3. *Times Literary Supplement*, May 7, 2004.

4. *The New Republic*, January 4, 2002.

5. *Philosophy and Public Affairs*, 36, no. 2 (2008).

6. *Philosophy and Public Affairs*, 33, no. 2 (2005).

7. *The New Republic*, June 27, 2005.

8. *The New Republic*, February 27, 2006.

9. *New York Review of Books*, May 25, 2006.

10. *Times Literary Supplement*, May 20, 2005.

11. *The New Republic*, October 21, 2002.

12. *London Review of Books*, May 11, 2006.

13. *Times Literary Supplement*, October 20, 2006.

14. *New York Review of Books*, April 11, 2002.

15. *Situating Sartre: The Florence Gould Lectures*, Winter 2006–2007.

Contents

PART I

Religion

I

Secular Philosophy and the Religious Temperament

[I]

Analytic philosophy as a historical movement has not done much to provide an alternative to the consolations of religion. This is sometimes made a cause for reproach, and for unfavorable comparisons with the continental tradition of the twentieth century, which did not shirk that task. That is one of the reasons that continental philosophy has been better received by the general public: It at least tries to provide nourishment for the soul, the job by which philosophy is supposed to earn its keep.

Analytic philosophers usually rebuff the complaint by pointing out that their concerns are continuous with the central occupations of Western philosophy from Parmenides onward: metaphysics, epistemology, logic, and ethical theory. Those topics have been pursued in a great tradition of works that are often technical and difficult, and that are not intended for a broad audience. The aim of that tradition is understanding, not edification.

This reply is formally correct, but it fails to acknowledge the significant element of yearning for cosmic reconciliation that has been part of the philosophical impulse from the beginning. Its greatest example is Plato, who had what I would call a profoundly religious temperament—displayed not in what he said about religion, but in his philosophy.

I am using the term "religious temperament" in a way that may seem illegitimate to those who are genuinely religious. Yet I think it is the appropriate name for a disposition to seek a view of the world that can play a certain role in the inner life—a role that for some people is occupied by religion.

Whether anything like this was part of the religion of fourth-century Athens I do not know. But Plato was clearly concerned not only with the state of his soul, but also with his relation to the universe at the deepest level. Plato's metaphysics was not intended to produce merely a detached understanding of reality. His motivation in philosophy was in part to achieve a kind of understanding that would connect him (and therefore every human being) to the whole of reality—intelligibly and, if possible, satisfyingly. He even seems to have suffered from a version of the more characteristically Judeo-Christian conviction that we are all miserable sinners, and to have hoped for some form of redemption from philosophy.

The desire for such completion, whether or not one thinks it can be met, is a manifestation of what I am calling the religious temperament. One way in which that desire can be satisfied is through religious belief. Religion plays many roles in human life, but this is one of them. I want to discuss what remains of the desire, or the question, if one believes that a religious response is not available, and whether philosophy can respond to it in another way.

I recognize that this is a conspicuously negative and roundabout way of identifying the subject: What, if anything, does secular philosophy have to put in the place of religion? One answer would be that nothing secular can be put in its place, either because there is something unreal about the question to which religion purports to provide the answer, or because it can be answered only in religious terms. But I do not think this is right. A space remains open if we deny that religion can make sense of everything. And one of the legitimate functions of philosophy is either to try to occupy that place or else to offer a way of assimilating the fact that nothing can occupy it. The subject overlaps with that of the meaning of life, but it is not the same. It is a question of making sense not merely of our lives, but of everything.

[II]

To better identify the question, we should start with the religious response. There are many religions, and they are very different, but what I have in mind is common to the great monotheisms, perhaps to some polytheistic religions, and even to pantheistic religions that don't have a god in the usual sense. It is the idea that there is some kind of all-encompassing mind or spiritual principle in addition to the minds of individual human beings and other creatures—and that this mind or spirit is the foundation of the existence of the universe, of the natural order, of value, and of our existence, nature, and purpose. The aspect of religious belief I am talking about is belief in such a conception of the universe, and the incorporation of that belief into one's conception of oneself and one's life.

The important thing for the present discussion is that if you have such a belief, you cannot think of yourself as leading a merely human life. Instead, it becomes a life in the sight of God, or an element in the life of the world soul. You must try to bring this conception of the universe and your relation to it into your life, as part of the point of view from which it is led. This is part of the answer to the question of who you are and what you are doing here. It may include a belief in the love of God for his creatures, belief in an afterlife, and other ideas about the connection of earthly existence with the totality of nature or the span of eternity. The details will differ, but in general a divine or universal mind supplies an answer to the question of how a human individual can live in harmony with the universe.

Perhaps religious persons will regard this as a simple-minded caricature, but it is the impression that a nonbeliever gets from the outside, of what it would be like to have a religious world view. In any case, I describe this impression in order to locate my topic, which is a question to which religion provides one type of answer. I want to know what becomes of the question if one does not give it a religious answer.

The question I have in mind is a general one about the relation of individual human life to the universe as a whole. The question is pointed to by its religious answer: namely, that our lives are in some way expressions or parts of the spiritual sense of the universe as a whole, which is its deepest reality, and that we must try to live them in light of this, and not only from the point of view of our local purely individual nature. I believe that the question to which this is one possible response remains to be asked, even if a religious response is not available, namely: How can one bring into one's individual life a recognition of one's relation to the universe as a whole, whatever that relation is?

It is important to distinguish this question from the pure desire for understanding of the universe and one's place in it. It is not an expression of curiosity, however large. And it is not the general intellectual problem of how to combine an objective conception of the universe with the local perspective of one creature within it. It is rather a question of attitude: Is there a way to live in harmony with the universe, and not just in it?

Without God, it is unclear what we should aspire to harmony with. But still, the aspiration can remain, to live not merely the life of the creature one is, but in some sense to participate through it in the life of the universe as a whole. To be gripped by this desire is what I mean by the religious temperament. Having, amazingly, burst into existence, one is a representative of existence itself—of the whole of it—not just because one is part of it but because it is present to one's consciousness. In each of us, the universe has come to consciousness, and therefore our existence is not merely our own.

To live not merely one's own life is also a demand of those forms of morality that take up a universal standpoint as part of their foundation. And something of the kind will very likely form part of a secular response to the religious question. But it is only a part, dealing specifically with recognition of the existence of other people. There is more to the question than this. The extrahuman world that contains and generates all these people also has a claim on us—a claim to be made part of our life. Existence is something tremendous, and day-to-day life, however indispensable, seems an insufficient response to it, a failure of consciousness. Outrageous as it sounds, the religious temperament regards a merely human life as insufficient, as a partial blindness to or rejection of the terms of our existence. It asks for something more encompassing, without knowing what that might be.

My subject is the secular philosophical responses to this impulse. I will (somewhat arbitrarily) call the question to which it seeks an answer the cosmic question. It is a question to which a religion could provide an answer, if one accepted it, but my discussion will concentrate on nonreligious responses. The question, again, is this: How can one bring into one's individual life a full recognition of one's relation to the universe as a whole? It is this quite general question, rather than the more specific search for redemption, that I will focus on.

The secular responses fall into three categories: (a) those that reject the question; (b) those that construct an answer from the inside out, that is, starting from the human point of view; and (c) those that construct an answer from the outside in, that is, starting from a cosmic point of view.

[III]

Let me begin by discussing the dismissive response that probably fits most comfortably with the analytic tradition. My impression is that most analytic philosophers are devoid of the religious temperament, and that they cannot take seriously the thought that something is missing if it is impossible to make sense of things in that way.[1] Sense, in this outlook, is something to be found within individual human lives, human creativity, human interactions, and human institutions. To take the quest for sense outside the boundaries of those human purposes and aims relative to which all judgments of sense or senselessness must be made is an error, and an error of a philosophically familiar type: an attempt to extend a concept beyond the conditions that give it meaning.

Among great philosophers of the past, I would particularly associate this outlook with Hume, who seems to me a beautiful example of someone perfectly free of religious impulses. His serene naturalism is a deep expression of his temperament, and he obviously feels no yearning for harmony with the cosmos.

This is certainly a possible secular stance: Take life as you find it, and try to play the hand you have been dealt by the contingencies of biology, culture, and history. It is possible to go far beyond these boundaries in the pursuit of pure understanding, but all such understanding will be essentially scientific. It isn't that there is a great absence of sense to the universe as a whole. It is just that there is no way for sense to be either present or absent at that level. And the sense that religious belief confers on everything is entirely gratuitous—an unnecessary add-on whose removal leaves no gap to be filled. If there were a god who was responsible for the existence of the universe and our place in it, the sense of everything would depend on him, but if there is no god, there is nothing by reference to which the universe can either have or lack sense.

Someone who takes this point of view can regard it as a legitimate philosophical task to try to make sense of human life from within—to have something systematic to say about the ends of life, the good life—the meaning of life in one sense of that expression. But it will not seem intelligible to try to make sense of human existence altogether.

This important outlook, probably dominant among atheists, places physical science at the top of the hierarchy of understanding for the universe as a whole. There are other kinds of understanding that are appropriate for local concerns at smaller and more intimate scales. But the universe revealed by chemistry and physics, however beautiful and awe-inspiring, is meaningless, in the radical sense that it is incapable of meaning. That is, natural science, as

---

1. The religious temperament is not common among analytic philosophers, but it is not absent. A number of prominent analytic philosophers are Protestant, Catholic, or Jewish, and others, such as Wittgenstein, clearly had a religious attitude to life without adhering to a particular religion. But I believe nothing of the kind is present in the makeup of Russell, Moore, Ryle, Austin, Carnap, Quine, Davidson, Strawson, or most of the current professoriate.

most commonly understood, presents the world and our existence as some-thing to which the religious impulse has no application. All we can do, and this is a great deal, is extend our knowledge of what the universe contains and of the laws that govern it.

This was not the outlook of religious scientists in the past, who saw them-selves as uncovering the wonders of God's creation. And some modern sci-entists, like Einstein, have taken a quasi-religious attitude toward the natural order and its intelligibility. But the most common secular attitude, I think, is that once we leave the human scale and move to the largest and most general theories, and ultimately perhaps to a theory of everything, we are in a realm of pure description.

One major intellectual task is to describe how the universe generated crea-tures that find themselves with the need to make some kind of sense of their lives. But this description itself does not have to make sense in the same way. It can be a purely factual account of how sense-seeking creatures—creatures like us, whose lives are capable of significant senselessness—emerged at a certain level of complexity of organization.

The point of the resolutely secular view is that there is nothing missing from this picture. When we look beyond the human world at the universe that contains it and has somehow given rise to it, we are not looking into the abyss. There is no need to carry on about the loneliness of man in the face of the vast impersonality of the universe, no need for the courage to forge a new destiny for ourselves after the death of God. That's just pretentious hand-wringing.

I have set out this view because it is the default or zero position to which I want to explore alternatives; we might call it affectless atheism, or hardheaded atheism. The universe exists and meets a certain description; one of the things it has generated is us; end of story. Of course, a new story begins with our exis-tence, since we find our own lives extraordinarily interesting. But this is a local phenomenon of perfectly understandable self-absorption, unconnected to the big picture. The big picture is of purely theoretical interest.

[IV]

It is a seductive position, and I do not doubt that many people find it comfort-able, as well as intellectually irresistible. To me, it has always seemed an eva-sion. It requires that we leave the largest question unanswered—in fact, that we leave it unasked, because there is no such question. But there is: It is the question "What am I doing here?" and it doesn't go away when science replaces a religious world view.

The question results from one of those steppings back that constitute the essence of philosophy. We find the familiar unfamiliar by reflecting on features of our situation, or forms of thought and action, so central and pervasive that we are ordinarily submerged in them without paying any notice. Philosophy in general is the most systematic form of self-consciousness. It consists in bringing to consciousness for analysis and evaluation everything that in ordinary life is invisible because it underlies and pervades what we are consciously doing.

In this case, the first thing that is brought to notice is that we are parts of the world. We wake up from our familiar surroundings to find ourselves, already elaborately formed by biology and culture, amazingly in existence, in the midst of the contingency of the world, and suddenly we do not know where we are or what we are. We recognize that we are products of the world and its history, generated and sustained in existence in ways we hardly understand, so that in a sense every individual life represents far more than itself. It is a short step, easily taken on a starry night, to thinking that one is a small representative of the whole of existence. That creates in susceptible minds the need to grasp that life and, if possible, to lead it as part of something larger—perhaps even as part of the life of the universe.[2]

So we wrench ourselves from the embedded familiarity of our surroundings and ask whether an understanding of the totality of which we are a part can in turn become part of the self-understanding by which we live. Can we to some extent encompass the universe that has produced us? Whether the answer is yes or no, and whether or not one takes any interest in it, the question, I believe, is real. So although we should keep in mind the default position of hardheaded atheism, according to which the scientific world view abolishes not only cosmic meaning but its absence, I want now to turn to less dismissive secular responses to the question.

[V]

The minimalist response is that the universe has nothing to offer that we can use, and that we are thrown back on our own resources.[3] This differs from

2. But see Conrad's sardonic observer Marlow for the opposite reaction: "It was one of those dewy, clear, starry nights, oppressing our spirit, crushing our pride, by the brilliant evidence of the awful loneliness, of the hopeless obscure insignificance of our globe lost in the splendid revelation of a glittering, soulless universe. I hate such skies." Joseph Conrad, *Chance*, Oxford World's Classics edition (Oxford: Oxford University Press, 2002), 41.

3. See Steven Weinberg: "The more the universe seems comprehensible, the more it also seems pointless." *The First Three Minutes* (New York: Basic Books, 1977), 155.

hardheaded atheism because it doesn't reject the question but tells us that we have to come to terms with our inability to answer it. We can't make sense of our lives from the point of view of our place in the universe, and shouldn't expect this to change even if we learn much more about the natural order. And that leaves a gap—the failure of a natural aspiration.

At this point, we may respond with either existentialist despair or existentialist defiance. The latter is particularly well expressed by Camus in *The Myth of Sisyphus*. It consists in making a virtue of the will to go on in spite of the complete indifference of the cosmos—without the kind of sense that religion could give to our lives. Not to be defeated by pointlessness is what gives our lives their point. That is as far as we can go toward living in light of our understanding of everything.

But there is another type of response that tries at least partially to fill the gap left by the death of God, working from the inside out. This is humanism, the view that we ourselves, as a species or community, give sense to the world as a whole. Human beings collectively can fill the place of the world soul. The significance of an individual life does depend on its embeddedness in something larger, but it is the collective consciousness of humanity rather than the cosmos that plays this role. Our self-consciousness and our place in cultural, cognitive, and moral history make membership in the human community a significant larger identity. The universe does not offer any sense to our lives, but we are not alone in it.

This response to the cosmic question does not show us how to live lives that are more than human, but it does argue that living a human life should be something much more than living the life of the individual human being one is. One should think of oneself as a representative of humanity, and live accordingly. Or perhaps a more substantive identity will involve one's particular place in history, and recognition of the origins of one's values and ties in a contingent historical genealogy.

A more abstract analogue of this universal self-conception is the foundation of Kant's moral theory, although Kant proposed that we should regard ourselves as representing the realm of all rational beings, not of anything so contingent and historical as the human species. A more humanist version of the Kantian conception is found in Rawls—see his evocation of the view sub specie aeternitatis at the end of *A Theory of Justice*.[4] Sidgwick's account of the

---

4. "The perspective of eternity is not a perspective from a certain place beyond the world, nor the point of view of a transcendent being; rather it is a certain form of thought and feeling that rational persons can adopt within the world. And having done so, they can, whatever their generation, bring together into one scheme all individual perspectives and arrive together at regulative principles that can be affirmed by everyone as he lives by them, each from his own standpoint. Purity of heart, if one could attain it, would be to see clearly and to act with grace and self-command from this point of view." Rawls, *A Theory of Justice* (Cambridge, Mass.: Harvard University Press, 1971), 587.

basis of utilitarianism, as an incorporation into our lives of the point of view of the universe, can be regarded as another example of cosmic sense constructed from inside out—since what the point of view of the universe endorses is an impartial concern for the happiness of all sentient creatures. Their individual lives remain the ultimate sources of value.

The thoughts that we should transcend the life of a particular person by taking on the value of humanity, or the value of all rational beings as ends in themselves, or the value of all sentient life, are partial answers to the cosmic question. They go part of the way toward incorporating a cosmic point of view into the life of the individual, and they certainly embed that life in something larger. But they stop with the value of human (and other) life itself, which does not receive endorsement from some higher value. The point of humanism and other "inside-out" answers is that no such endorsement or external support is needed. It is we who give sense to the universe, so there is no need for a higher principle to give sense to us.

Another example is Sartre's existentialism: "There is no universe other than a human universe, the universe of human subjectivity,"[5] he says, summing up his argument that existentialism is a form of humanism. He interprets humanism through a somewhat unstable doctrine of radical freedom constrained by universal prescriptivism: Since God does not exist, everything is permitted, but in choosing what to be, I must think of myself as choosing for everyone. This shares with other humanisms the principle that we are the source of all value, which replaces the value not given to our lives by the nonexistent creator.

William James says, "Were one asked to characterize the life of religion in the broadest and most general terms possible, one might say that it consists of the belief that there is an unseen order, and that our supreme good lies in harmoniously adjusting ourselves thereto."[6] Humanism denies this, and finds our supreme good in harmony not with an unseen but with a visible order—one that is universal in a sense, but not unduly unfamiliar.

[VI]

Humanism and its relatives take us outside of ourselves in search of harmony with the universe, but not too far outside. Since the universe cannot be identified with the human world, they do not really give us a way of incorporating

5. Jean-Paul Sartre, *L'existentialisme est un humanisme* (1946) (Paris: Gallimard, 1996), 76; translated by Bernard Frechtman, *Existentialism* (New York: Philosophical Library, 1947), 60.

6. William James, *The Varieties of Religious Experience* (New York: Longmans, Green and Co., 1902) (Dover reprint, 2002), 53.

our conception of the universe as a whole into our lives and how we think of them. Because they take conscious life as a self-contained source of value, their cosmic ambition is limited. In a way, it is more limited than the forms of existentialism that require us to live in the acknowledgment that our lives are senseless, and that there is no harmony possible for us. But perhaps a more ambitious form of harmony, grounded in a larger view of our place in the universe, can be constructed on a secular basis. That is the project of "outside-in" responses to the cosmic question.

When we travel further outside the human perspective than even the universal value of humanity, or of rational or sentient beings, we come to the natural order. The scientific conception of that order is uncompromisingly secular. The question we now have to ask is whether it provides a naturalistic view of our relation to the universe that can be taken on as an essential part of the standpoint from which we lead our lives. Remember, we are talking about possible secular answers to the cosmic question, not about ways of rejecting the question. The development of a naturalistic account of the universe and our appearance in it can be a purely intellectual project, and hardheaded atheism says it has nothing to do with how we are to live—even though scientific knowledge about ourselves may be useful in enabling us to live longer and better. But I am asking now whether it can do something more, namely, provide us with a way of seeing the point or sense of our lives from a perspective larger than the human one from which we naturally start.

The most likely candidate for such a perspective is that of biology, in particular the evolutionary biology of our epoch. More fundamental sciences like physics and chemistry, even though we fall under them, don't seem to offer a perspective from which life can be lived. But biology may, and the evolutionary perspective toward ourselves can seem to offer the possibility of a transformative self-conception—one that is larger than even the universal human perspective.

Evolutionary theory is at the heart of contemporary philosophical naturalism about language, thought, perception, value, ethics, and action, but it often has nothing to do with the cosmic question or the religious temperament. Often, of course, it is associated with the rejection of religion, of its aspirations, and of anything resembling them.

But there is another strain of evolutionary naturalism that can be thought of as a replacement for religion. Its greatest representative is Nietzsche. What is distinctive about Nietzsche is that he turns a genealogical self-understanding, based on both biology and history, into a highly individual project of self-creation. He does not think that an understanding of his place in the natural order leads to moral universalism or anything similar. Instead, he thinks it should lead to freedom from the flattening influence of collective values and collective ideas.

Yet this is pursued in the name of a still larger framework, that of the great biological struggle that is responsible for one's existence and of which one's life is a part.[7] Our freedom and capacity for self-creation depends on our capacity to understand the evolutionary sources of the multiple and conflicting drives that constitute us—sources in both biological and social evolution. The revaluation of values that is Nietzsche's project starts from the values that have been bred into us by our species and its cultural history. The meaning of those values can be understood only through their genealogy—by understanding the functions they performed that led to their survival.

Only on the basis of such genealogical self-understanding can we re-create ourselves—not with the absolute freedom of Sartre's existentialism but by a reordering of our existing drives through a process of lifelong self-selection that is itself a form of evolution. "Valuing freely, as self selecting one's values, is precisely to value in the light of an understanding of why one values. It is to 'incorporate' insight into the selective processes—Darwinian and cultural— that made the values of one's body and spirit."[8] Once we understand how humans have come to be "the sick animal," the animal in which the products of natural and social selection are in conflict, we can in full consciousness re-create ourselves to transcend this conflict. (There is a distinct resemblance here to Freud's diagnosis of the human condition in *Civilization and Its Discontents*, but Freud is much more pessimistic than Nietzsche about the possible extent of our recaptured freedom.)

As Richardson observes, Nietzsche is so multifaceted that one can at best say that the Darwinian theme is one aspect of his views. But exegetical questions aside, this way of understanding and living one's life does seem an important form of naturalistic response to the cosmic question: How can one live in light of an understanding of the universe and one's place in it?

Instead of starting from one's existing values, one steps back and tries first to understand them in virtue of one's place in a much larger natural and historical order, and then to recast one's life from this new, expanded starting point. Nietzsche's ethical and political conclusions are famously radical, but I won't consider them here. It is the general strategy of importing not just historical genealogy but evolutionary biology into the perspective from which one lives that is significant. Nietzsche offers this as a source of enlarged meaning,

---

7. For this reading of Nietzsche, I am indebted to John Richardson's perceptive study, *Nietzsche's New Darwinism* (New York: Oxford University Press, 2004).

8. Richardson, 107.

which replaces the illusory meaning of religion and conventional morality. It is therefore a response to the cosmic question that is distinct from religion, from humanism, and from existentialism.

But can naturalism play this role? How much of one's genealogical, biological, and evolutionary identity does it make sense to assume as one's point of view? A certain measure of such identification is an important antidote to excessive spiritualization. The idea that we humans are really immortal souls temporarily trapped in animal bodies is no longer very attractive, but it has been in the past, and resistance to it has been important in the thought both of Nietzsche and of Freud. Our animality and its history are important aspects of the self that has been built up over eons of genealogical descent. We should not try to escape living our animal life, nor regard it just as a necessary platform for keeping afloat the real life of the higher faculties.

This is not yet a response to the cosmic question. It is a somewhat expanded or enriched conception of our humanity, rather than an expansion of our perspective to include a relation to the universe. But in Nietzsche's case, the connection between evolution and the will to power as the universal explanatory principle makes Darwinism more than a merely biological form of self-understanding. Nietzsche's philosophy is a secular response to the cosmic question, because it tells us how to live on the basis of a comprehensive understanding of our existence as an expression of the fundamental forces of nature. To be sure, what Nietzsche offers in his writings is a very individual response, one that depends specifically on Nietzsche's place in the history of humanity, which he believes gives him a unique understanding of the human genealogy and a unique capacity to make his own life the site for a revaluation of all values that can usher in the next stage of human evolution. But he clearly hoped to offer a choice that others might take up.

For most of us, however, the recognition that we are the products of biological and cultural evolution does not give us a task, a significant role in this larger process. The genealogical facts are interesting, and may lead to some significant self-conscious modifications of what we have been given, but for the most part we take what has resulted from the process as our starting point and live from there forward. Each of us is only a small drop in the evolutionary and historical river. Even if we recognize the importance of our origins to self-awareness, it is hard to see ourselves as expressions of the will to power. Modern evolutionary self-understanding is typically more passive than that.[9]

---

9. The use of genealogy to vindicate, rather than undermine, a fundamental human value has recently been proposed by Bernard Williams in his book *Truth and Truthfulness: An Essay in Genealogy* (Princeton, N.J.:

[VII]

There is a general reason to think that evolutionary naturalism cannot provide a response to the cosmic question. Nietzsche's conception of evolution, with his underlying power ontology, is very different from the modern Darwinian consensus. As it is usually understood, evolutionary naturalism is radically antiteleological. This implies that it is not suited to supply any kind of sense to our existence, if it is taken on as the larger perspective from which life is lived. Instead, the evolutionary perspective probably makes human life, like all life, meaningless, since it makes life a more or less accidental consequence of physics.

If that is so, then any response to the cosmic question will have to come from within the perspective of human life rather than from the evolutionary perspective toward it. This leads us back either to some form of humanism, to existentialist absurdity, or more likely to hardheaded atheism—the view that there is no way of making the scientific understanding of our place in the universe part of the sense of our lives, and that it doesn't matter.

Darwin's theory of evolution on its own does not have this consequence, because Darwin recognized that it did not explain the origin of life—only the origin of species through natural selection once life and biological heredity were in existence. But the evolutionary naturalism of our day is usually associated with an assumption that both the course of evolution and the origin of life have their basic explanation in the nonbiological sciences, even if the details of that explanation remain to be discovered.

The profoundly nonteleological character of this modern form of naturalism is concealed by the functional explanations that fill evolutionary accounts of the characteristics of living organisms. But any reference to the function or survival value of an organ or other feature is shorthand for a long story of purposeless mutations followed, because of environmental contingencies, by differential reproductive fitness—survival of offspring or other relatives with the same genetic material. It is in the most straightforward sense false that we have eyes in order to see and a heart to pump the blood. Darwinian natural

---

Princeton University Press, 2002). Williams believes that history, rather than pure philosophy, provides the enlarged view needed to transcend the unreflective individual perspective—though I should add that Williams, in spite of his admiration for Nietzsche, is quite free of the religious temperament. His humanism is not intended to fill a gap left by the death of God, and he is happy to dismiss the view sub specie aeternitatis as irrelevant to human concerns. See his remarkable essay on humanism, "The Human Prejudice," in his *Philosophy as a Humanistic Discipline* (Princeton, N.J.: Princeton University Press, 2006).

selection could be compatible with teleology if the existence of DNA had the purpose of permitting successive generations of organisms to adapt through natural selection to changes in the environment—but that, of course, is not the naturalistic conception.

That conception, far from offering us a sense of who we are, dissolves any sense of purpose or true nature that we may have begun with. The meaning of organic life vanishes in the meaninglessness of physics, of which it is one peculiar consequence. It is widely thought that, without knowing the details, we now have every reason to believe that life arose from a lifeless universe, in virtue of the basic laws of particle physics or string theory or something of the kind, which did not have life or us "in mind." Hence the description of these ultimate laws as a theory of everything. Hence also the grateful remark of Richard Dawkins that Darwin made it possible for the first time to be an intellectually fulfilled atheist.[10]

A genealogy of this kind gives us nothing to live by. As Daniel Dennett says, it is "universal acid: it eats through just about every traditional concept."[11] To live, we must fall back on our contingently formed desires, reserving the scientific world picture for intellectual and instrumental purposes. If naturalism means that everything reduces to physics, then there is no naturalistic answer to the cosmic question. So the next question is whether there is any secular alternative to this kind of reductive naturalism.

[VIII]

There may be the radical alternative of some kind of Platonism, according to which there is a nonaccidental fit between us and the world order: In other words, the natural order is such that, over time, it generates beings that are both part of it and able to understand it. Such a nonreductionist conception, though teleological, does not postulate intention or purpose behind one's existence and relation to the universe. Still, it would repudiate the essentially mechanistic conception of nature that has dominated modern thought in the scientific age. I believe there are reasons to doubt the capacity of that conception to account for everything about us, and therefore for everything about the universe. That is not enough by itself to support a Platonist alternative, but if Platonism could be reconciled with the facts, it would offer some sense of what

---

10. Richard Dawkins, *The Blind Watchmaker* (New York: W. W. Norton, 1986), 6.
11. Daniel Dennett, *Darwin's Dangerous Idea* (New York: Simon and Schuster, 1995), 63.

we are that can be internalized in a way that the reductionist, cosmic accident picture cannot. Each of us, on this view, is a part of the lengthy process of the universe gradually waking up. It was originally a biological evolutionary process, and in our species, it has become a collective cultural process as well. It will continue, and seen from a larger perspective, one's own life is a small piece of this very extended expansion of organization and consciousness.

Human life, too, though it is the most advanced version we know of, is only a part of the process. So the identification it encourages is not a form of humanism. In some respects, this is a return to the Nietzschean conception of mere humanity as a stage that we may be in a position to transcend. At the same time, it would share the Nietzschean identification with the prehuman sources that remain embedded in our present nature. We are bound up in many ways with life in general and are ourselves animals, as both Nietzsche and Freud emphasized.

But does it really make any difference whether we are the products of natural teleology or of pure chance? Without an intentional designer, perhaps there is no sense to be made of our lives from the larger perspective in either case: We just have to start from what we contingently are and make what sense we can of our lives from there.

If the question is about whether our lives have a cosmic purpose, I would agree. But that is not the only possibility. The Platonic sense of the world is that its intelligibility and the development of beings to whom it is intelligible are nonaccidental, so our awareness and its expansion as part of the history of life and of our species are part of the natural evolution of the cosmos. This expands our sense of what a human life is. It seems in that case at least somewhat less plausible to say that all sense begins with the contingent desires and choices of the particular individual—that existence precedes essence, in the existentialist formula.

In the Platonic conception, even the biological and cultural evolution that has led to the starting point at which each of us arrives on Earth and reaches consciousness is embedded in something larger, something that makes that entire history less arbitrary than it is on the reductive view. But if the Platonic alternative is rejected along with the religious one, we must go back to the choice between hardheaded atheism, humanism, and the absurd. In that case, since the cosmic question won't go away and humanism is too limited an answer, a sense of the absurd may be what we are left with.

2

Dawkins and Atheism

Richard Dawkins, the most prominent and accomplished scientific writer of our time, is convinced that religion is the enemy of science. Not just fundamentalist or fanatical or extremist religion, but all religion that admits faith as a ground of belief and asserts the existence of God. In *The God Delusion*[1] he attacks religion with all the weapons at his disposal, and as a result the book is a very uneven collection of scriptural ridicule, amateur philosophy, historical and contemporary horror stories, anthropological speculations, and cosmological scientific argument. Dawkins wants both to dissuade believers and to embolden atheists.

Since he is operating mostly outside the range of his scientific expertise, it is not surprising that *The God Delusion* lacks the superb instructive lucidity of his books on evolutionary theory, such as *The Selfish Gene*, *The Blind Watchmaker*, and *Climbing Mount Improbable*. In this new book I found that kind of pleasure only in the brief explanation of why the moth flies into the candle flame—an example introduced to illustrate how a useful trait can have disastrous side effects. (Dawkins believes the prevalence of religion among human beings is a side effect of the useful trust of childhood.)

One of Dawkins's aims is to overturn the convention of respect toward religion that belongs to the etiquette of modern civilization. He does this by persistently violating the convention, being as offensive

1. Richard Dawkins, *The God Delusion* (New York: Houghton Mifflin, 2006).

as possible, and pointing with gleeful outrage at absurd or destructive religious beliefs and practices. This kind of thing was done more entertainingly by H. L. Mencken (whom Dawkins quotes with admiration), but the taboo against open atheistic scorn seems to have become even more powerful since Mencken's day. Dawkins's unmitigated hostility and quotable insults—"The God of the Old Testament is arguably the most unpleasant character in all of fiction"— will certainly serve to attract attention, but they are not what make the book interesting.

The important message is a theoretical one, about the reach of a certain kind of scientific explanation. At the core of the book, in a chapter entitled "Why There Almost Certainly Is No God," Dawkins sets out with care his position on a question whose importance cannot be exaggerated—the question of what explains the existence and character of the astounding natural order we can observe in the universe we inhabit. On one side is what he calls "the God Hypothesis," namely: "there exists a superhuman, supernatural intelligence who deliberately designed and created the universe and everything in it, including us." On the other side is Dawkins's alternative view: "any creative intelligence, of sufficient complexity to design anything, comes into existence only as the end product of an extended process of gradual evolution. Creative intelligences, being evolved, necessarily arrive late in the universe, and therefore cannot be responsible for designing it." In Dawkins's view the ultimate explanation of everything, including evolution, lies in the laws of physics, which explain the laws of chemistry, which explain the existence and functioning of those self-replicating molecules that underlie the biological process of genetic mutation and natural selection.

This pair of stark alternatives may not exhaust the possibilities, but it poses the fundamental question clearly. In the central argument of the book, the topic is not institutional religion or revealed religion, based on scripture, miracles, or the personal experience of God's presence. It is what used to be called "natural religion," or reflection on the question of the existence and nature of God using only the resources of ordinary human reasoning. This is not the source of most religious belief, but it is important nonetheless.

In an earlier chapter Dawkins dismisses with contemptuous flippancy the traditional a priori arguments for the existence of God offered by Aquinas and Anselm. I found these attempts at philosophy, along with those in a later chapter on religion and ethics, particularly weak; he seems to have felt obliged to include them for the sake of completeness. But his real concern is with the argument from design, because there the conflict between religious belief and atheism takes the form of a scientific disagreement—a disagreement over the most plausible explanation of the observable evidence. He argues that contemporary science gives us decisive reason to reject the argument from design, and to regard the existence of God as overwhelmingly improbable.

The argument from design is deceptively simple. If we found a watch lying on a deserted heath (William Paley's famous example), we would conclude that such an intricate mechanism, whose parts fit together to carry out a specific function, did not come into existence by chance, but that it was created by a designer with that function in mind. Similarly, if we observe any living organism, or one of its parts, such as the eye or the wing or the red blood cell, we have reason to conclude that its much greater physical complexity, precisely suited to carry out specific functions, could not have come into existence by chance, but must have been created by a designer.

The two inferences seem analogous, but they are very different. First, we know how watches are manufactured, and we can go to a watch factory and see it done. But the inference to creation by God is an inference to something we have not observed and presumably never could observe. Second, the designer and the manufacturer of a watch are human beings with bodies, using physical tools to mold and put together its parts. The supernatural being whose work is inferred by the argument from design for the existence of God is not supposed to be a physical organism inside the world, but someone who creates or acts on the natural world while not being a part of it.

The first difference is not an objection to the argument. Scientific inference to the best explanation of what we can observe often leads to the discovery of things that are themselves unobservable by perception and detectable only by their effects. In that sense, God might be no more and no less observable than an electron or the Big Bang. But the second difference is more troubling, since it is not clear that we can understand the idea of purposive causation—design— by a nonphysical being on analogy with our understanding of purposive causation by a physical being such as a watchmaker. Somehow the observation of the remarkable structure and function of organisms is supposed to lead us to infer as their cause a disembodied intentional agency of a kind totally unlike any that we have ever seen in operation.

Still, even this difference need not be fatal to the argument, since science often concludes that what we observe is to be explained by causes that are not only unobservable, but totally different from anything that has ever been observed, and very difficult to grasp intuitively. To be sure, the hypothesis of a divine creator is not a scientific theory with testable consequences independent of the observations on which it is based. And the purposes of such a creator remain obscure, given what we know about the world. But a defender of the argument from design could say that the evidence supports an intentional cause of some kind, and that it is hardly surprising that God, the bodiless designer, while to some extent describable theoretically and detectable by his effects, is resistant to full intuitive understanding.

Dawkins's reply to the argument has two parts, one positive and one negative. The positive part consists in describing a third alternative, different from both chance and design, as the explanation of biological complexity. He agrees that the eye, for example, could not have come into existence by chance, but the theory of evolution by natural selection is capable of explaining its existence as due neither to chance nor to design. The negative part of the argument asserts that the hypothesis of design by God is useless as an alternative to the hypothesis of chance, because it just pushes the problem back one step. In other words: Who made God? "A designer God cannot be used to explain organized complexity because any God capable of designing anything would have to be complex enough to demand the same kind of explanation in his own right."

Let me first say something about this negative argument. It depends, I believe, on a misunderstanding of the conclusion of the argument from design, in its traditional sense as an argument for the existence of God. If the argument were supposed to show that a supremely adept and intelligent natural being, with a super-body and a super-brain, is responsible for the design and creation of life on earth, then of course this "explanation" would be no advance on the phenomenon to be explained. If the existence of plants, animals, and people requires explanation, then the existence of such a super-being would require explanation for exactly the same reason. But if we consider what that reason is, we will see that it does not apply to the God hypothesis.

The reason we are led to the hypothesis of a designer by considering both the watch and the eye is that these are complex physical structures that carry out a complex function, and we cannot see how they could have come into existence out of unorganized matter purely on the basis of the purposeless laws of physics. For the elements of which they are composed to have come together in just this finely tuned way purely as a result of physical and chemical laws would have been such an improbable fluke that we can regard it in effect as impossible: The hypothesis of chance can be ruled out. But God, whatever he may be, is not a complex physical inhabitant of the natural world. The explanation of his existence as a chance concatenation of atoms is not a possibility to which we must find an alternative, because that is not what anybody means by God. If the God hypothesis makes sense at all, it offers a different kind of explanation from those of physical science: explanation by the purpose or intention of a mind without a body, capable nevertheless of creating and forming the entire physical world. The point of the hypothesis is to claim that not all explanation is physical, and that there is a mental, purposive, or intentional explanation more fundamental even than the basic laws of physics, because it explains even them.

All explanations come to an end somewhere. The real opposition between Dawkins's physicalist naturalism and the God hypothesis is a disagreement over whether this end point is purely physical, extensional, and purposeless, or whether it is mental, intentional, and purposive. On either view, the ultimate explanation is not itself explained. The God hypothesis does not explain the existence of God, and naturalistic physicalism does not explain the laws of physics.

This entire dialectic leaves out another possibility, namely, that there are teleological principles in nature that are explained neither by intentional design nor by purposeless physical causation—principles that therefore provide an independent end point of explanation for the existence and form of living things. That, more or less, is the Aristotelian view that was displaced by the scientific revolution. Law-governed causation by antecedent conditions became the only acceptable form of scientific explanation, and natural tendencies toward certain ends were discredited. The question then became whether nonteleological physical law can explain everything, including the biological order.

Darwin's theory of natural selection offered a way of accounting for the exquisite functional organization of organisms through pure physical causation, an explanation that revealed it to be the product neither of design nor of hopelessly improbable chance. This is the positive part of Dawkins's argument. The physical improbability of such complexity's arising can be radically reduced if it is seen as the result of an enormous number of very small developmental steps, in each of which chance plays a part, together with a selective force that favors the survival of some of those forms over others. This is accomplished by the theory of heritable variation, due to repeated small mutations in the genetic material, together with natural selection, due to the differential adaptation of these biological variations to the environments in which they emerge. The result is the appearance of design without design, purely on the basis of a combination of physical causes operating over billions of years.

This is only the schema for an explanation; most of the details of the story can never be recovered, and there are many issues among evolutionary biologists over how the process works. There are also skeptics about whether such a process is capable, even over billions of years, of generating the complexity of life as it is. But I will leave those topics aside, because the biggest question about this alternative to design takes us outside the theory of evolution.

It is a question that Dawkins recognizes and tries to address, and it is directly analogous to his question for the God hypothesis: "Who made God?" The problem is this. The theory of evolution through heritable variation and natural selection reduces the improbability of organizational complexity by breaking the process down into a very long series of small steps, each of which is not all that improbable. But each of the steps involves a mutation in a carrier of genetic information—an enormously complex molecule capable both of precise self-replication and of generating out of surrounding matter a functioning organism that can house it. The molecule is moreover capable sometimes of surviving a slight mutation in its structure to generate a slightly different organism that can also survive. Without such a replicating system, there could not be heritable variation, and without heritable variation, there could not be natural selection favoring those organisms, and their underlying genes, that are best adapted to the environment.

The entire apparatus of evolutionary explanation therefore depends on the prior existence of genetic material with these remarkable properties. Since 1953 we have known what that material is, and scientists are continually learning more about how DNA does what it does. But because the existence of this material or something like it is a precondition of the possibility of evolution, evolutionary theory cannot explain its existence. We are therefore faced with a problem analogous to that which Dawkins thinks faces the argument from design: We have explained the complexity of organic life in terms of something that is itself just as functionally complex as what we originally set out to explain. So the problem is just pushed back one step: How did such a thing come into existence?

Of course, there is a huge difference between this explanation and the God hypothesis: We can observe DNA and see how it works. But the problem that originally prompted the argument from design, namely, the overwhelming improbability of such a thing coming into existence by chance, simply through the purposeless laws of physics, remains just as real for this case. Yet this time we cannot replace chance with natural selection.

Dawkins recognizes the problem, but his response to it is pure handwaving. First, he says it only had to happen once. Next, he says that there are, at a conservative estimate, a billion billion planets in the universe with life-friendly physical and chemical environments like ours. So all we have to suppose is that the probability of something like DNA forming under such conditions, given the laws of physics, is not much less than one in a billion billion. And he points out, invoking the so-called anthropic principle, that even if it happened on only one planet, it is no accident that we are able to observe it, since the appearance of life is a condition of our existence.

Dawkins is not a chemist or a physicist. Neither am I, but general expositions of research on the origin of life indicate that no one has a theory that would support anything remotely near such a high probability as one in a billion billion. Naturally, there is speculation about possible nonbiological chemical precursors of DNA or RNA. But at this point the origin of life remains, in light of what is known about the huge size, the extreme specificity, and the exquisite functional precision of the genetic material, a mystery—an event that could not have occurred by chance and to which no significant probability can be assigned on the basis of what we know of the laws of physics and chemistry.

Yet we know that it happened; that is why the argument from design is still alive, and why scientists who find the conclusion of that argument unacceptable feel there must be a purely physical explanation of why the origin of life is not as physically improbable as it seems. Dawkins invokes the possibility that there are vastly many universes besides this one, thus giving chance many more opportunities to create life, but this looks like a desperate device to avoid the demand for a real explanation.

I agree with Dawkins that the issue of design versus purely physical causation is a scientific question. He is correct to dismiss Stephen J. Gould's position that science and religion are "non-overlapping magisteria"—the conflict is real. But although I am as much of an outsider to religion as he is, I believe it is much more difficult to settle the question than he thinks. I also suspect that there are other possibilities besides these two that have not even been thought of yet. The fear of religion leads too many scientifically minded atheists to cling to a defensive, world-flattening reductionism. Dawkins, like many of his contemporaries, is hobbled by the assumption that the only alternative to religion is to insist that the ultimate explanation of everything must lie in particle physics, string theory, or whatever invariant spatiotemporal laws govern the elements of which the material world is composed.

This reductionist dream is nourished by the extraordinary success of the physical sciences, not least in their recent application to the understanding of life through molecular biology. It is natural to try to take any successful intellectual method as far as it will go. Yet the impulse to find an explanation of everything in physics has over the last fifty years got out of control. The concepts of physical science provide a very special, and partial, description of the world that experience reveals to us. It is the world with all subjective consciousness, sensory appearances, thought, value, purpose, and will left out; what remains is the mathematically describable order of things and events in space and time.

That conceptual purification launched the extraordinary development of physics and chemistry that has taken place since the seventeenth century. But reductive physicalism turns this description into an exclusive ontology. The reductionist project usually tries to reclaim some of the originally excluded aspects of the world, by analyzing them in physical (e.g., behavioral or neurophysiological) terms, but it denies reality to what cannot be so reduced. I believe the project is doomed—that conscious experience, thought, value, and so forth are not illusions, even though they cannot be identified with physical facts.

I also think there is no reason to undertake the project in the first place. We have more than one form of understanding. Different forms of understanding are needed for different kinds of subject matter. The great achievements of physical science do not make it capable of encompassing everything, from mathematics to ethics to the experiences of a living animal. We have no reason to dismiss moral reasoning, introspection, or conceptual analysis as ways of discovering the truth, just because they are not physics.

Any antireductionist view leaves us with very serious problems about how the mutually irreducible types of truths about the world are related. At least part of the truth about us is that we are physical organisms composed of ordinary chemical elements. If thinking, feeling, and valuing aren't merely complicated physical states of the organism, what are they? What is their relation to the brain processes on which they seem to depend? More: If evolution is a purely physical causal process, how can it have brought into existence conscious beings?

A religious world view is only one response to the conviction that the physical description of the world is incomplete. Dawkins says with some justice that the will of God provides a too easy explanation of anything we cannot otherwise understand, and therefore brings inquiry to a stop. Religion need not have this effect, but it can. More reasonable, in my estimation, would be to admit that we do not now have the understanding or knowledge on which to base a comprehensive theory of reality.

Dawkins seems to believe that if people could be persuaded to give up the God Hypothesis on scientific grounds, the world would be a better place not just intellectually but morally and politically. He is horrified—as who cannot be?—by the dreadful things that continue to be done in the name of religion, and he argues that the sort of religious conviction that includes a built-in resistance to reason is the true motive behind many of them. But there is no connection between the fascinating philosophical and scientific questions posed by the argument from design and the attacks of September 11. Blind faith and the authority of dogma are dangerous; the view that we can make ultimate sense of the world only by understanding it as the expression of mind or purpose is not. It is unreasonable to think that one must refute the second in order to resist the first.

3

Why Is There Anything?

The question "Why is there something rather than nothing?" provoked one of Sidney Morgenbesser's memorable comebacks: "If there was nothing, you'd still be complaining!" Bede Rundle's response in *Why There Is Something Rather Than Nothing*[1] is somewhat longer but just as uncompromising. He argues that the question is ill-formed because there could not have been nothing. He offers general reflections on causality, eternity, God, mind, matter, and agency in order to evaluate the idea that the existence of anything at all, while it cannot be explained by science, might be explained by theology. His strategy is to argue in detail that the question, and the attempts to answer it, consistently take language beyond the bounds of meaningfulness, detaching familiar words from their usual conditions of application so that they no longer express intelligible possibilities. He is following the method of Wittgenstein, as he conceives it, though with results more destructive to religious language than Wittgenstein's own view.

The linguistic transgressions that Rundle finds fall into three categories: the idea of God, ideas of causality and explanation, and ideas about existence. They appear in the thought that, though science can explain what goes on in the universe by discovering the systematic connections among its features and elements, the existence of the

---

1. Bede Rundle, *Why There Is Something Rather Than Nothing* (Oxford: Oxford University Press, 2004).

universe as a whole clearly cannot be explained in this way, so we must seek an explanation of it in something that is not part of the universe, but outside of space and time. And if that explanation is not to leave us with a further demand to explain the existence of what we have identified as the ultimate cause, then that cause has to be something whose existence doesn't require explanation— something that couldn't not exist. This role has traditionally been attributed to God.

It is important that in talking about the existence of the universe, Rundle is not using the term "universe" in the peculiar way that is now common, to mean a particular cosmic entity that might be only one of many such entities, either coexisting or succeeding one another. In this recent sense of the term, it is possible to say that our universe—the one we live in—came into existence with the Big Bang, but that this was perhaps preceded by the contraction of a prior universe into the concentrated point from which the Big Bang exploded, or that it perhaps arose from a black hole in another universe.

In this sense, the existence of our universe might be explained by scientific cosmology, but such an explanation would still have to refer to features of some larger reality that contained or gave rise to it. A scientific explanation of the Big Bang would not be an explanation of why there was something rather than nothing, because it would have to refer to something from which that event arose. This something, or anything else cited in a further scientific explanation of it, would then have to be included in the universe whose existence we are looking for an explanation of when we ask why there is anything at all. This is a question that remains after all possible scientific questions have been answered.

Rundle dismisses as incoherent the idea that it could be answered by the hypothesis that God created the universe at some time in the past. He says that this tries to employ the idea of an agent producing something, while withholding two of the crucial conditions of the concept of agency: time and physical causation. We can understand the idea of God molding Adam out of clay, but the idea that a nonphysical God whose existence is neither in space nor in time might cause space and time to start to exist at a certain point simply takes the idea of cause and agency off the rails. A nonspatiotemporal being, if there could be such a thing, couldn't do anything.

Much of Rundle's discussion has this down-to-earth, commonsense flavor: Look at the ordinary way we use the terms "cause" or "mind" or "exist" or "nothing," and you'll see that in theological speculation they are being used in a way that tears them loose from these familiar conditions without supplying anything in their place. The minds we can talk about are revealed in what people with bodies do in space and time. When a mental intention brings something about, it is through intentional physical action in an already existing world. The problem Rundle finds with most theological claims is not that they are unverifiable, but that they are unintelligible. He goes on to say, however, that even if we reject the thought that God might have brought the universe into existence in the past, there remains another version of the question that seems to require an answer.

> The universe may neither have, nor be susceptible of, a causal expla-
> nation, but the why-question seemingly remains. Not "Why does it
> exist?" where a cause of becoming is sought, but "Why does it exist?"
> where the query is motivated by considerations of modality: the
> universe need not have existed, surely, so the fact that it does is a fact
> that calls for explanation.

Even if God did not create the universe from nothing in the past, perhaps he sustains the universe in existence at all times, preventing the fall into nothingness.

It is this possibility of absolute nothingness that Rundle is mainly concerned to expose as an illusion. He points out that in ordinary speech, when we say there is nothing in the cupboard, or nothing that is both round and square, we are talking about an existing world, none of whose contents meet a certain description. To say nothing is X is to say everything is not X. We can perhaps conceive of the disappearance of everything in the world, so that there are no things left in it, but even then we are not imagining nothing at all, but rather a void, a vacuum, empty space. Taken literally, the hypothesis that there might have been nothing at all seems self-contradictory, since it seems equivalent to the supposition that it might have been the case that nothing was the case. Is there any way of understanding the possibility that there might have been nothing at all without interpreting it incoherently as a way things might have been—a fact, as Rundle puts it, a possible state of affairs, an alternative possible world? Rundle thinks not, and that therefore the question "Why is there something rather than nothing?" does not call for an answer.

Even if it is inconceivable that nothing whatever should exist, it doesn't follow that there is any particular entity whose existence is necessary. Yet Rundle has a view about the kind of thing that has to exist: not God, but matter. He is not a materialist, for he doesn't think all other kinds of truths are equivalent to physical truths. But he does hold that our mental and mathematical concepts, for example, though not definable in physical terms, depend for their application on features of the physical world. "The thesis that nothing can exist in the absence of a material universe does not imply the nonsensical view that everything is material, but we can hold that if anything exists, matter exists, on the grounds that it is only in matter that the necessary independent existence is to be found." One consequence is that "if there is no place for immaterial agents, then there is no place for God."

Even if one does not accept many of Rundle's Wittgensteinian interpretations of the way ordinary language works—interpretations that depend heavily on conditions of assertability available to the speaker—he has offered a serious challenge to the intelligibility of what is widely regarded as a fundamental question, as well as to one type of answer. And he does not admit the saving position that Wittgenstein himself apparently favored—that religious language does not make factual claims at all, but rather expresses an attitude toward the world. But it will not come as news to those who believe that God is responsible for the existence of the universe that they are not using words in the sense they bear in their ordinary worldly context. As Rundle acknowledges, claims about the attributes and acts of God are supposed to be based on a very distant analogy with what is meant by "mind," "good," "cause," or "create" in ordinary speech, and it is thought that we cannot grasp the divine nature but only gesture toward it with such analogical language. He rejects this kind of meaning as an illusion.

The most difficult philosophical question posed by Rundle's critique is whether such efforts to use words to indicate something that transcends the conditions of their ordinary application make sense. This question is especially acute with regard to the why-question itself, which is immediately gripping even to people who find a theological response ineligible for reasons like Rundle's. Though it is likely to make you giddy, it is hard to cast off the thought that there might have been nothing at all—not even space and time—that nothing might have been the case, ever. It is not a thought of how things might have been. It is not the thought of an empty universe. Nevertheless, it seems an alternative to all the possible positive ways the world could have been—an alternative both to the actual universe and to all the other possible universes that might have existed instead, each of them crammed with facts.

Perhaps each of us can imagine it on the analogy of our own nonexistence. The possibility that you should never have been born is an alternative to all the alternative possible courses of your experiential life, as well as to your actual life. From the objective point of view, of course, this is a perfectly imaginable state of affairs, but it is not an alternative possible course of experience for you: Subjectively, it would be not something different, but nothing. The possibility that there should never have been anything at all is the objective analogue to the subjective possibility—all too real, when you think about it—that you should never have existed.

While it is risky to use existing language to reach beyond its existing limits, we are impelled to do so again and again, however inadequately, in our recognition that our understanding of reality is so limited. This applies also to the question "Why?" which we seem capable of raising about anything, even if we have no idea what would count as an answer. Rundle's book is a wonderful stimulus to reflect on the ways in which philosophy can and cannot identify the excesses of attempted thought.

4

Nietzsche's Self-Creation

[I]

Most people take life as they find it, and try to make something of the possibilities that are offered by their personal and social circumstances, avoiding catastrophe or failure, pursuing happiness, and working to realize some acceptable private or public ambitions. A small minority have the leisure to devote themselves systematically to understanding life and the world: scientists, historians, and thinkers. Others, seeing that there is much that is wrong with the world, spend their lives trying to change it for the better, and not just for themselves. Still others, creative artists, try to add to the world wonders that do not yet exist. Friedrich Nietzsche's conception of his own task, the task of the true philosopher, was closest to the last of these—not merely to understand the world or to change it, but to create something new. And the field of his creation was himself.

To take oneself and one's world as given, and move forward intellectually and practically from that starting point, was in his view a betrayal of the extraordinary freedom we have as reflective beings. Nietzsche recognized that, like all human beings, he had reached consciousness with a sense of himself and a system of values that was produced by a tangled human history, together with biological sources of which he was largely unaware. To take real possession of himself, to discover who he was and decide who he wanted to be, required a bringing to consciousness of everything that lay beneath and behind the socially developed and educated human being—the constructed individual who handles the world with concepts, values, and methods of thought whose sources and true meaning he does not understand. It required a radical self-transformation.

Nietzsche's assault on the familiar is more radical even than Descartes' skepticism. Descartes believed that by doubting everything he had learned in the ordinary way, he would find within himself an unassailable form of thought that would allow him to reconstruct his knowledge on a secure foundation, so that he would no longer be just the accidental product of a contingent culture. But Nietzsche found no such thing in himself. He was as suspicious of reason and the concepts of the understanding as other philosophers had been of the senses. The operations of the mind, he believed, are not necessarily what they seem.

This does not mean that greater self-knowledge is impossible: Indeed, plunging beneath your own inner surface through both psychological and historical investigation is essential. But knowledge is not the main point. The point is to achieve a different kind of existence: to live one's life in the full complexity of what one is, which is something much darker, more contradictory, more of a maelstrom of impulses and passions, of cruelty, ecstasy, and madness, than is apparent to the civilized being who glides on the surface and fits smoothly into the world. Because we are not animals, we are in a position to take conscious possession of ourselves in this way, but because we are socialized human beings, we tend instead to accept the superficial identities and the orderly system of beliefs that civilization has assigned to us.

[II]

Rüdiger Safranski's life of Nietzsche[1] concentrates on the temporal course of Nietzsche's inner life and his self-transformation through thought and writing. References to outer events are all subordinate to this aim, and the basic chronology is given not in the main text but in an appendix. The last chapter is a valuable account of the afterlife of Nietzsche's ideas, which have had an influence on modern thought comparable to those of Marx, Darwin, and Freud. A few personal relations are part of the story, but readers interested in juicy details will not find them here. This is a book about what was really important to Nietzsche: the largely solitary attempt to live up to the recognition that existence is something tremendous.

---

1. Rüdiger Safranski, *Nietzsche: A Philosophical Biography*, translated by Shelley Frisch (New York: W. W. Norton, 2002).

Safranski covers the full range of Nietzsche's writings, making use of new critical editions, including the complete *Nachlass*, the letters, and the early writings. Covering so much, he does not give special emphasis to the topics that are of most interest to contemporary academic philosophy—truth, objectivity, and skepticism about morality—but the result is a balanced and illuminating intellectual and spiritual portrait, and a guide to the writings, published and unpublished, that should interest scholars as well as a general audience.

The outer facts of Nietzsche's life are these. Born in 1844, the son of a Protestant pastor, he lost his father at the age of five. He was precocious, and wrote nine autobiographical sketches during his school and university years, trying to understand his development, as well as ambitious essays to formulate his philosophical and historical ideas. At the unheard-of age of twenty-four, even before receiving his doctorate, he was appointed professor of classical philology at the University of Basel on account of his evident brilliance. He became a fervent disciple of Wagner, and published *The Birth of Tragedy* at twenty-seven, thereby antagonizing the classical profession. He resigned his professorship on grounds of chronic illness at twenty-eight, with a pension of three thousand Swiss francs a year. From then until his irreversible collapse into dementia in January 1889, he moved from place to place, mostly in Switzerland and Italy, mostly alone, fighting illness, publishing books and filling notebooks in a crescendo of ecstatic and uninhibited brilliance.

Personally, his life was marked by a turning against Wagner, by aversion to his mother and sister, and by a painful relation with the beautiful and brilliant Lou Salomé, who returned his fascination but rejected his offers of marriage and eventually drew away from him. (He then described her in a letter as "This scrawny dirty smelly monkey with her fake breasts—a disaster!") As a published author, he was not a success: After he had been writing books steadily for fifteen years, only about five hundred copies all told of his works had been sold.

Not quite as bad a fate as Van Gogh's, but close. It was only after he couldn't appreciate it that his books began to sell, and at the beginning of the First World War, one hundred fifty thousand copies of *Thus Spoke Zarathustra* were printed in a special edition and distributed to soldiers at the front, along with Goethe's *Faust* and the New Testament. After his breakdown, the publication of his works was taken in charge by his anti-Semitic sister, Elisabeth. He died in August 1900. Though he seems to have had a very limited sexual life, the cause of his illness and death is generally thought to have been syphilis.

[III]

The sense of a deep connection with reality has often been given religious expression, but in light of the spreading modern recognition that God is dead—that religion is a human creation rather than a transcendent truth—Nietzsche looked for something to replace it that was not merely banal, not merely a scientific worldview. As Lou Salomé observed, there was something religious in his temperament.

Nietzsche found that music had the power to bring him into direct contact with reality—that the experience of music brought something deeper than words and rational understanding could provide. No distance or observation or description separates us from music. In the form of music, the deepest reality penetrates us, and we become conscious parts of it. This is a recognizable feeling; it is somehow appropriate that Stanley Kubrick employs the explosive opening of Richard Strauss's *Thus Spoke Zarathustra* in *2001: A Space Odyssey* to evoke the birth of human consciousness. Nietzsche's first hope, that music combined with a new and unchristian mythology would allow us to connect with the deeper reality not expressed in modern or scientific discourse, was inspired by the works of Richard Wagner, which he found ecstatically moving, and it was given expression in *The Birth of Tragedy*.

The ancient Greeks had practically invented rationality, but Nietzsche argued that in their art a detached or Apollonian grasp of the world had existed side by side with the conflicting, passionate, Dionysian force of unreflective being. Apollo was the god of clarity and form, Dionysus the god of orgiastic ecstasy. Nonrational and potentially destructive feeling contained by, but always threatening to burst the bounds of, self-reflective rational control and understanding: This was the drama of human life, raised to a high level in Greek tragedy. But the subordination of art by the triumph of reason had led in the modern world to a loss of contact with the Dionysian sources of life, and something needed to be done to revive them.

Yet when Nietzsche witnessed the opening in 1876 of the first Bayreuth Festival, blessed by the appearance of the Kaiser and thronged with prosperous spectators, and saw Wagner's fawning response to all this worldly attention, he was repelled. He concluded that a reenchantment of the world by new collective myths was not the answer. It was too much like religion. But the need remained to bring out the Dionysian forces without taming them, and this was Nietzsche's artistic and philosophical project for the rest of his short productive life.

It meant probing what lay beneath the surface of consciousness in his own psyche, as well as critical examination, on both historical and psychological grounds, of the customary forms of thought and justification that are imposed on us without our consent or even our awareness. Most famously, it meant calling into question morality, whose sources were very poorly understood—asking for the significance of morality, as he put it, from the perspective of life. What we need, he said, is not the courage of our convictions, but the courage for an attack on our convictions.

Nietzsche was a prodigious source of ideas, too many and too contradictory to sum up, but the most important strain in his thought, I believe, was suspicion of the authority exercised by collective, supposedly objective or rational norms and concepts over the individual perspectives and drives at the core of life. And his characteristic method of calling that authority into question was to unmask the claim of objectivity and impersonality as itself the expression of an individualized drive—in the most general terms, the will to power, power over the world and over others.

The conflict of perspectives and competing wills that is the true reality is obscured and flattened out by the social imposition of a common standpoint, in language, thought, morality, and politics, which presents itself as simply or cosmically true by concealing its true sources. The inquiry into the genealogy of these ruling ideas is therefore a vital part of their unmasking. The proposed genealogy of Christian morality, as the expression not of universal love but of the slave revolt of the base against the noble, motivated by fear, hatred, and envy, is Nietzsche's most famous thesis, expounded in *Beyond Good and Evil* and *On the Genealogy of Morals*. As Safranski puts it, "The battle in morality boils down to the power of definition. It is ultimately a question of who allows himself to be judged by whom."

Not all expressions of the will to power can be rejected on the ground that they conceal their true sources. Some perspectives achieve dominance over others not by deception but because of their greater strength. Thus Nietzsche was not a skeptic about the value of science as a way of going beyond the appearances; he was skeptical only of its pretensions to offer the ultimate view of the world, to which all other perspectives must be subordinated. He diagnosed this as the expression of an ascetic ideal, an attempt to eliminate the multiple and unruly individual forces of life in favor of a spare objective order.

He regarded modern morality, which speaks with the voice of the community or even of humanity as a whole, as particularly dangerous, because it requires suppression of the cruelty and recklessness that distinguish the strong individual. The height of self-realization cannot be reached by someone who is too concerned with the reactions of others, or his effects on them. There is a fundamental conflict between the pursuit of individual creativity and perfection and the claims of the general welfare.

For this reason, Nietzsche was not a democrat. Already at the time of writing *The Birth of Tragedy*, he defended slavery as a condition of the possibility of great cultural achievement by the few, as in ancient Athens. And he defended its modern counterpart, the economic oppression of the masses, for the same reason. He opposed shortening the workday from twelve hours to eleven when it was proposed in Basel, he approved of child labor, and he opposed educational groups for workers. When in 1871 he heard the false rumor that the Paris communards had pillaged the Louvre, he called it "the worst day of my life." Equality meant nothing to him; he believed it would inevitably push everything down to the lowest common denominator, that of the "democratic herd animal." Life, he insisted, is tragic; it is necessary to choose between justice and aesthetic perfection. And in his latest writings he expressed fantasies of annihilation, with "degenerates" being got rid of to make room for the highest type of man.

The figure who embodied his hopes was the *Übermensch*, not to be confused with his virtuous comic-strip namesake. The *Übermensch* is a possible successor to man, self-created by bringing to consciousness all the strong and contradictory forces that lie beneath the human surface, acknowledging the omnipresence of the will to power, and revaluing all existing values, through assessment of their genealogies, from the perspective of this enlarged acceptance of life. It is doubtful that anything like morality would survive for such a creature, but if so, it would have to take a form that can be affirmed in this way.

There is a final element of the overall conception to which Nietzsche assigned supreme importance—the puzzling idea of eternal recurrence. On August 6, 1881, Nietzsche was inspired, apparently with the help of defective mathematical reasoning, to the insight that the entire history of the universe, including his own life, had already happened an infinite number of times and would repeat itself infinitely into the future. (The trouble with the argument is that even if we grant that time is infinite and the number of possible states of the universe is finite, it follows only that some of those states will repeat infinitely often, not that all of them will.)

Apart from the question of its truth, why did Nietzsche think this idea so important? Safranski is right, I think, to hold that it provided him with a form of sanctification of life without religion, for it made every moment of life eternal. The past has not ceased to exist, and the present is not vanishing as we live through it. Every moment of our being is real forever. And the *Übermensch* is the being whose capacity for self-affirmation will enable him to rejoice at this thought.

[IV]

Nietzsche is so complex that he can be invoked in support of many outlooks, some of them brutal or nihilistic. The Nazis certainly found him encouraging, in spite of the fact that he was an outspoken anti-anti-Semite and an enemy of German chauvinism who would have despised Nazism as an extreme manifestation of the herd instinct. He is also sometimes regarded as a destroyer of the idea of truth and a prophet of postmodernism, though it is clear that he utterly rejected the notion that all perspectives are equal—and that he had at the least a robust sense of falsehood, which is difficult to separate from some conception of truth. One of the most interesting things about Nietzsche is his attempt to challenge the claims of objectivity as the privileged route to truth, without falling into nonjudgmental relativism. Whether his perspectivism permits this reconstitution of truth on a new footing continues to be debated by readers of Nietzsche, but Safranski does not say much about these semantic and epistemological subtleties.

On the positive side, Safranski finds a recurrent theme of support for what he calls bicameral thinking, the claim that a higher culture must give people, as Nietzsche says,

> two chambers of the brain, as it were, one to experience science and the other non-science: lying juxtaposed, without confusion, divisible, able to be sealed off; this is necessary to preserve health. The source of power is located in one region; the regulator, in the other. Illusions, partialities, and passions must provide the heat, while the deleterious and dangerous consequences of overheating must be averted with the aid of scientific knowledge.[2]

Safranski comments: "The idea of a bicameral system flashes up again and again in Nietzsche's work and then vanishes, much to the detriment of his philosophy. If he had held to it, he might well have spared himself some of his mad visions of grand politics and the will to power." As this suggests, the idea has moral as well as epistemological implications, even if Nietzsche did not draw them. The potentially anarchic will of the individual, which provides the heat of life, need not be destroyed by the acceptance of norms of justice and impartiality that incorporate the combined viewpoints of many individuals and

2. Nietzsche, *Human, All Too Human*, sec. 251.

attempt to reconcile them. An egalitarian morality need not crush individual freedom and creativity; it can be liberal, thus transcending the purchase of the freedom of the few at the price of the slavery of the many.

This, too, the desire to live on mutually acceptable terms with our fellow humans, is a deep part of us, and here I would say that Kant had more self-understanding than Nietzsche, who felt the point of view of the other as an invasion from without. As often happens, the inebriating sense of power to unmask illusions gave rise in his case to illusions of its own.

Safranski ends with the image of Caspar David Friedrich's painting *The Monk by the Sea*—the individual in the face of immensity. "Kant," he says, "had asked whether we ought to leave the terra firma of reason and venture out into the open sea of the unknown. Kant had advocated remaining here. Nietzsche, however, ventured out." We can be grateful for what he found on the journey and recognize that he invented new forms of self-examination that are now common property. At the same time we should distrust as signs of weakness his inflated heroics of rebellion, pitiless cruelty, and daring in the face of the abyss. And this is as it should be, for Nietzsche did not attempt to produce a system fully defended against attack, but rather a method of attack that should work even against himself.

5

Public Education and Intelligent Design

[I]

The 2005 decision by Judge John E. Jones in *Kitzmiller v. Dover Area School District* was celebrated by all red-blooded American liberals as a victory over the forces of darkness. The result was probably inevitable, in view of the reckless expression by some members of the Dover School Board of their desire to put religion into the classroom and the clumsiness of their prescribed statement in trying to dissimulate that aim.[1] But the conflicts aired in this trial—over the status of evolutionary theory, the arguments for intelligent design, and the

---

1. The whole case was about the following text, which was to be read to students in ninth-grade biology class:

The Pennsylvania Academic Standards require students to learn about Darwin's Theory of Evolution and eventually to take a standardized test of which evolution is a part.

Because Darwin's Theory is a theory, it continues to be tested as new evidence is discovered. The Theory is not a fact. Gaps in the Theory exist for which there is no evidence. A theory is defined as a well-tested explanation that unifies a broad range of observations.

Intelligent Design is an explanation of the origin of life that differs from Darwin's view. The reference book, *Of Pandas and People*, is available for students who might be interested in gaining an understanding of what Intelligent Design actually involves.

With respect to any theory, students are encouraged to keep an open mind. The school leaves the discussion of the Origins of Life to individual students and their families. As a Standards-driven district, class instruction focuses upon preparing students to achieve proficiency on Standards-based assessments. (*Kitzmiller v. Dover Area Sch. Dist.*, 400 F. Supp. 2d 707 (M.D. Pa. 2005), at pp. 708–709)

nature of science—reveal an intellectually unhealthy situation. The political urge to defend science education against the threats of religious orthodoxy, understandable though it is, has resulted in a counterorthodoxy, supported by bad arguments, and a tendency to overstate the legitimate scientific claims of evolutionary theory. Skeptics about the theory are seen as so dangerous, and so disreputably motivated, that they must be denied any shred of legitimate interest. Most important, the campaign of the scientific establishment to rule out intelligent design as beyond discussion because it is not science results in the avoidance of significant questions about the relation between evolutionary theory and religious belief, questions that must be faced in order to understand the theory and evaluate the scientific evidence for it.

It would be unfortunate if the Establishment Clause made it unconstitutional to allude to these questions in a public school biology class, for that would mean that evolutionary theory cannot be taught in an intellectually responsible way. My aim is to address the constitutional issue, but first I want to discuss the relation between evolutionary theory and the despised alternative. For legal reasons, that alternative is called intelligent design, with no implication that the designer is God, but I shall assume that we are talking about some form of divine purpose or divine intervention. Nevertheless, there is a distinction between the arguments for intelligent design in biology and the traditional argument from design for the existence of God. Intelligent design (ID, as I shall call it, in conformity to current usage) is best interpreted not as an argument for the existence of God, but as a claim about what it is reasonable to believe about biological evolution if one independently holds a belief in God that is consistent both with the empirical facts about nature that have been established by observation and with the acceptance of general standards of scientific evidence. For legal reasons, it is not presented that way by its defenders, but I think that is a mistake.

From the beginning, it has been commonplace to present the theory of evolution by random mutation and natural selection as an alternative to intentional design as an explanation of the functional organization of living organisms. The evidence for the theory is supposed to be evidence for the absence of purpose in the causation of the development of life forms on this planet. It is not just the theory that life evolved over billions of years, and that all species are descended from a common ancestor. Its defining element is the claim that all this happened as the result of the appearance of random and purposeless mutations in the genetic material, followed by natural selection due to the resulting heritable variations in reproductive fitness. It displaces design by proposing an alternative.

No one suggests that the theory is not science, even though the historical process it describes cannot be directly observed but must be inferred from currently available data. It is therefore puzzling that the denial of this inference—that is, the claim that the evidence offered for the theory does not support the kind of explanation it proposes, and that the purposive alternative has not been displaced—should be dismissed as not science. The contention seems to be that, although science can demonstrate the falsehood of the design hypothesis, no evidence against that demonstration can be regarded as scientific support for the hypothesis. Only the falsehood, and not the truth, of ID can count as a scientific claim. Something about the nature of the conclusion, that it involves the purposes of a supernatural being, rules it out as science.

The problem cannot be just that the idea of a designer is too vague, and that nothing is being said about how he works. When Darwin proposed the theory of natural selection, neither he nor anyone else had any idea of how heredity worked, or what could cause a mutation that was observable in the phenotype and was heritable. The proposal was simply that something purposeless was going on that had these effects, permitting natural selection to operate. This is no less vague than the hypothesis that the mutations available for selection are influenced by the actions of a designer. So it must be the element of purpose that is the real offender.

I believe there is a reason for this, and that it depends on a premise that, though completely valid, does not have the consequences that are usually drawn from it. The premise is that the purposes and actions of God, if there is a god, are not themselves, and could not possibly be, the object of a scientific theory in the way that the mechanisms of heredity have become the object of a scientific theory since Darwin. We do not have much scientific understanding of the creative process even when the creator is human; perhaps such creativity, too, is beyond the reach of science. Leaving that aside: The idea of a divine creator or designer is clearly the idea of a being whose acts and decisions are not explainable by natural law. There is no divine scientific psychology.

So the purposes and intentions of God, if there is a god, and the nature of his will are not possible subjects of a scientific theory or scientific explanation. But that does not imply that there cannot be scientific evidence for or against the intervention of such a non-law-governed cause in the natural order. The fact that there could be no scientific theory of the internal operation of the divine mind is consistent with its being in large part a scientific question whether divine intervention[2] provides a more likely explanation of the empirical data than an explanation in terms of physical law alone. To ask whether there are limits to what can credibly be explained by a given type of

---

2. I shall use the term "intervention" to cover any kind of intentional influence, whether during the course of evolution or in the creation of the initial conditions that led to it.

scientific theory, or any theory relying only on universal physical laws, is itself a scientific question. An answer to the question that asserts such limits on the basis of empirical evidence is still a scientific claim, even if it also proposes an alternative cause whose internal operation is not governed by the kind of natural law that science can investigate. I suspect that the assumption that science can never provide evidence for the occurrence of something that cannot be scientifically explained is the principal reason for the belief that ID cannot be science; but so far as I can see, that assumption is without merit.

I assume it will be granted by everyone that, even though the past cannot be directly observed, a scientific argument against the Darwinian theory of evolution is not impossible. If it were impossible, that would cast doubt on whether the theory is itself science. The theory makes claims about the causes of evolution that are inferred from the available evidence and that could be undermined by further evidence. For example, as we learn more about the behavior of the genetic material, and more about how the properties of organisms depend on it, it will be possible to give more precise answers to questions about the rate at which viable mutations can occur randomly as a result of physical accident, the kinds of phenotypic changes they can generate, and the number of generations within which specific changes would have had to occur to make the theory fit the development of organisms as we know them. Together with calculations of the numbers of individual organisms that have been involved in the major transitions in evolution, this should make it possible to evaluate the theory mathematically.

Most evolutionary biologists are confident about the answers to these questions, but there is no a priori guarantee that they will eventually be answered in a way that confirms the theory. One of the disturbing things about the public debate is that scientists engaged in it sometimes write as if the idea of fundamental problems with the theory (as opposed to problems of detail in its application) were unthinkable, and that to entertain such doubts is like wondering whether the earth is flat. This seems to me, as an outsider, a vast underestimation of how much we do not know, and how much about the evolutionary process remains speculative and sketchy. Since it is a scientific theory that makes large claims about what cannot be directly observed, there could be scientific evidence against it (and new evidence is constantly becoming available in this case, since molecular biology is so new).

There is one question whose legitimacy is particularly important for our purposes: whether the mutations on which natural selection has operated are entirely due to chance. Is this question decisively settled in the affirmative by the available evidence, or can a reasonable observer regard it as still open? Marc W. Kirschner and John C. Gerhart, who reject ID but who present a naturalistic theory of "facilitated variation" in their book, *The Plausibility of Life*, put the problem as follows:

> In evolution, selection always acts on variation of the *phenotype*, which includes all the observable and functional features of the organism.... Selection does not directly act on the DNA sequence (also called the *genotype*).... The question unanswered by the two well-established pillars of evolutionary theory (selection and heredity) is whether, given the rate and nature of changes in the DNA, *enough of the right kind* of phenotypic variation will occur to allow selection to do its work, powering complex evolutionary change.... Is genetic variation purely random, or is it in fact biased to *facilitate* evolutionary change?[3]

Stuart Kauffman, a complexity theorist who defends a naturalistic theory of emergence, says this:

> I propose that much of the order in organisms may not be the result of selection at all, but of the spontaneous order of self-organized systems.... The order of organisms is natural, not merely the unexpected triumph of natural selection.... Evolution is not merely "chance caught on the wing," in Monod's evocative image. The history of life captures the natural order, on which selection is privileged to act.[4]

Are the sources of genetic variation uniformly random or not? That is the central issue, and the point of entry for defenders of ID. In his recent book, *The Edge of Evolution*, Michael Behe examines a body of currently available evidence about the normal frequency and biochemical character of random mutations in the genetic material of several organisms: the malaria parasite, the human immunodeficiency virus (HIV), the bacterium *E. coli*, and humans. He argues that those widely cited examples of evolutionary adaptation, including the development of immunity to antibiotics, when properly understood, cannot be extrapolated to explain the formation of complex new biological systems. These, he claims, would require mutations of a completely different order, mutations whose random probability, either as simultaneous multiple mutations or as sequences of separately adaptive individual mutations, is vanishingly small. He

---

3. Marc W. Kirschner and John C. Gerhart, *The Plausibility of Life* (New Haven, Conn.: Yale University Press, 2005), 12–13. They believe that facilitated variation, although nonrandom, is itself the product of earlier natural selection.

4. Stuart Kauffman, *At Home in the Universe* (New York: Oxford University Press, 1995), 25.

concludes that "alterations to DNA over the course of the history of life on earth must have included many changes that we have no statistical right to expect, ones that were beneficial beyond the wildest reach of probability."[5]

Like Kauffman, he believes that random mutation is not sufficient to explain the range of variation on which natural selection must have acted to yield the history of life: Some of the variation was not due to chance. This seems on the face of it to be a scientific claim about what the evidence suggests, and one that is not self-evidently absurd. I cannot evaluate it; I merely want to stress its importance for the current debate. Skepticism about the standard evolutionary model is not limited to defenders of ID. The skeptics may be right, or they may be wrong. But even if one merely regards the randomness of the sources of variation as an open question, it seems to call for the consideration of alternatives.

[II]

The claim that ID is not a scientific theory implies that even if there were scientific evidence against evolutionary theory, which was originally introduced as an alternative to design, that would not constitute any scientific evidence for ID. We might have to give up evolutionary theory, but then we would be constrained by the canons or definition of science to look for a different scientific, that is, nonpurposive, explanation of the development of life, because science prohibits us from even considering ID as a possible alternative explanation, one whose eligibility would otherwise be enhanced by the rejection of the leading scientific explanation, namely, evolutionary theory.

What would it take to justify the claim that there are propositions such that the discovery of evidence against them can qualify as science, but evidence in favor of them cannot? Someone who accepts this view would probably extend it to propositions about ghosts or extrasensory perception. Research showing that effects that some benighted souls have attributed to ghosts or mental telepathy can be explained in a perfectly naturalistic way would count as science, but any argument that the evidence does not support those explanations, and that significant experimental or observational data are better explained by ghosts or by ESP, would not count as science and could therefore be ruled out of consideration. On this view it would not even be a false scientific claim.

The idea is that any naturalistic or nonspiritual explanation of a phenomenon can be either confirmed or disconfirmed by empirical evidence, together

5. Michael Behe, *The Edge of Evolution* (New York: Free Press, 2007), 165.

with causal and probabilistic reasoning. No empirical evidence against such a nonspiritual alternative, however, nor any other kind of empirical evidence, could provide a reason for believing the spiritual hypothesis. Belief in something like that is necessarily the result of a different cognitive process, having nothing to do with the scientific evaluation of empirical evidence (rank superstition or blind faith, to give it its true name). I submit that this way of drawing the boundaries around science depends not on a definition but on the unspoken assumption that all such propositions are obviously false—there are no ghosts, there is no ESP, and there is no god—so that to invoke such things to explain any observed phenomenon, even one for which no other explanation is available, reveals a disposition to take seriously a possibility that a rational person would not consider. Without this assumption, the exclusion of ID from consideration cannot be defended.

In order to think that the refutation or very low probability of all the available alternatives provides support for an explanation E of some observation, one has to believe that E is at least possible. So if one thinks that the existence of ghosts is not a possibility, no spooky manifestations, however elaborate and otherwise inexplicable, will be taken as evidence, however weak, that a ghost is behind them. The real issue over the scientific status of ID is over what determines the antecedent belief in the possibility that a nonphysical being should intervene in the natural order. Opponents of the scientific status of ID are moved by the fact that those who believe this is possible, and who therefore can regard certain empirical observations as evidence for its actuality, usually believe in the possibility as a result of faith or ecclesiastical authority, rather than evidence. This nonscientific element, which is a necessary condition of their interpretation of the empirical evidence, is thought to undermine the scientific status of the whole position.

Unfortunately, it also seems to undermine the scientific status of the rejection of ID. Those who would not take any amount of evidence against evolutionary theory as evidence for ID, like those who would not take evidence against naturalistic explanations of spooky manifestations as evidence for the presence of a ghost, seem to be assuming that ID is not a possibility. What is the status of that assumption? Is it scientifically grounded?[6] It may not be a matter of faith or ecclesiastical authority, but it does seem to be a basic, ungrounded assumption about how the world works, essentially a kind of naturalism. If it operates as an empirically ungrounded boundary on the range of possibilities that can

6. An exclusionary assumption clearly can be scientifically grounded. For example, the existence of ghosts can be disregarded as a possibility in light of the consistently negative findings of the Society for Psychical Research during the nineteenth century. Of course, some people would find it reasonable to rule out ghosts, like God, even without such evidence.

be considered in seeking explanations of what we can observe, why does that not undermine the scientific status of the theories that depend on it, just as much as a somewhat different assumption about the antecedent possibilities?

It is often said that this particular set of boundaries is just part of the definition of science. I suspect that this simply reflects the confusion pointed out earlier: the assumption that there cannot be a scientific argument for the presence of a cause that is not itself governed by scientific laws. In any event, a purely semantic classification of a hypothesis or its denial as belonging or not to science is of limited interest to someone who wants to know whether the hypothesis is true or false. He will be interested in evaluating both the scientific evidence for its falsehood and the evidence, whatever it may be called, for its truth (which would have to include arguments against the adequacy of the scientific evidence for its falsehood). The objector's claim is not just terminological: It is that in view of the basis of a belief in design, it has no right to be considered in competition with naturalistic accounts of the same subject matter, by those seeking to explain what is observed.

The denier that ID is science faces the following dilemma. Either he admits that the intervention of such a designer is possible, or he does not. If he does not, he must explain why that belief is more scientific than the belief that a designer is possible. If, on the other hand, he believes that a designer is possible, then he can argue that the evidence is overwhelmingly against the actions of such a designer, but he cannot say that someone who offers evidence on the other side is doing something of a fundamentally different kind. All he can say about that person is that he is scientifically mistaken.

Similar things could be said about differences in antecedent belief that assigned higher or lower probabilities, rather than just possibility and impossibility, to the existence of a designer. If these prior probabilities have a large effect on the interpretation of the empirical evidence, and if neither of them is empirically based, it is hard to imagine that one of them should render the resulting reasoning unscientific whereas the other does not.

I think there are only two possible justifications for this asymmetry. Either there is strong scientific evidence against the existence of God, or there is a scientific default presumption that the prior probability of a designer is low, and the only possible basis for assigning it a higher probability—high enough to make it eligible as an explanation of what is empirically observed—is faith, revelation, or ecclesiastical authority. Is either of those things true, however? Is the opposition between these prior probabilities really an opposition between scientific rationality and unreasoned dogmatism?[7]

7. Judge Jones adopted the position urged on him by expert witnesses for the plaintiffs, that the exclusion of purposive explanation is just one of the ground rules of science:

It seems to me that in this respect ID is very different from young earth creationism and the "creation science" that it spawned. There are people who believe, on the authority of the Bible, that God created the earth and all the creatures on it about six thousand years ago. The fact that this proposition is inconsistent with various scientific theories of cosmology, geology, and biology does not make it a scientific claim.

Biblical literalism is not a scientific hypothesis because it is not offered as an explanation of the empirical evidence, but is accepted as a divine revelation. So long as no observations about the natural world are offered in its support, it is not even a false scientific claim. When, however, in response to the finding that the teaching of creationism in public schools was unconstitutional, the producers of creation science tried to argue that young earth creationism was consistent with the geological and paleontological evidence, they succeeded in putting forward a scientific claim, even though their reason for doing so was that they believed it to be true on other grounds, and their arguments were easily refuted.[8] A scientific hypothesis can be false and unsupported by the evidence. That is a good enough reason not to teach it to schoolchildren. It is not necessary to argue that it is not science, not even hopelessly bad science.

Intelligent design is very different from creation science. To an outsider, at least, it does not seem to depend on massive distortion of the evidence and hopeless incoherencies in its interpretation. Nor does it depend, like biblical literalism, on the assumption that the truth of ID is immune to empirical evidence to the contrary. What it does depend on is the assumption that the hypothesis of a designer makes sense and cannot be ruled out as impossible or assigned a vanishingly small probability in advance. Once it is assigned a significant prior probability, it becomes a serious candidate for support by empirical evidence, in particular empirical evidence against the sufficiency of standard evolutionary theory to account for the observational data. Critics take issue with the claims made by defenders of ID about what standard evolutionary mechanisms can accomplish, and argue that they depend on faulty assumptions. Whatever the

---

This rigorous attachment to "natural" explanations is an essential attribute to science by definition and by convention. We are in agreement with Plaintiffs' lead expert Dr. Miller, that from a practical perspective, attributing unsolved problems about nature to causes and forces that lie outside the natural world is a "science stopper." As Dr. Miller explained, once you attribute a cause to an untestable supernatural force, a proposition that cannot be disproven, there is no reason to continue seeking natural explanations as we have our answer. (*Kitzmiller*, at p. 736)

Yet the idea that someone who admits the possibility of design as an explanation will have no reason to look for explanations in terms of natural law is completely unsupported, either epistemologically or historically. From Newton on down, scientists who believe in God have always been as intent as anyone else to discover universal natural laws that can be empirically confirmed.

8. See Philip Kitcher, *Abusing Science: The Case against Creationism* (Cambridge, Mass.: MIT Press, 1982).

merits, however, that is clearly a scientific disagreement, not a disagreement between science and something else.

A great deal therefore hangs on the sources of differences between investigators in their attitude to this prior probability, and the relevance of those sources to the scientific character of their convictions. It is difficult to avoid the conclusion that the two sides are in symmetrical positions. If one scientist is a theist and another an atheist, this is either a scientific or a nonscientific disagreement between them. If it is scientific (supposing this is possible), then their disagreement is scientific all the way down. If it is not a scientific disagreement, and if this difference in their nonscientific beliefs about the antecedent possibilities affects their rational interpretation of the same empirical evidence, I do not see how we can say that one is engaged in science and the other is not. Either both conclusions are rendered nonscientific by the influence of their nonscientific assumptions, or both are scientific in spite of those assumptions.

In the latter case, they have a scientific disagreement that cannot be settled by scientific reasoning alone. The same could be said of a disagreement between two theists, one of whom considers divine tinkering in the natural order a possibility and the other of whom does not. Kenneth Miller, the leading scientific witness against intelligent design in the Dover case, is apparently an example of the latter. He is a Catholic, but his conception of God's relation to the creation is incompatible with intervention in the evolutionary process.[9] That is part of his religious outlook, not a scientific belief, but it has consequences for his scientific interpretation of the evidence, specifically for his confidence that traditional evolutionary explanations exist for the development of the most complex biological systems, whether we are able to discover them or not.

I agree with Philip Kitcher that the response of evolutionists to creation science and intelligent design should not be to rule them out as "not science." He argues that the objection should rather be that they are bad science, or dead science: scientific claims that have been decisively refuted by the evidence.[10] That would certainly be enough to rule out their being discussed in science

---

9. "In obvious ways, the various objections to evolution take a narrow view of the capabilities of life—but they take an even narrower view of the capabilities of the Creator. They hobble His genius by demanding that the material of His creation ought not to be capable of generating complexity. They demean the breadth of His vision by ridiculing the notion that the materials of His world could have evolved into beings with intelligence and self-awareness. And they compel Him to descend from heaven onto the factory floor by conscripting His labor into the design of each detail of each organism that graces the surface of our living planet" (Kenneth Miller, *Finding Darwin's God* [New York: HarperCollins, 1999], 268).

10. Philip Kitcher, *Living with Darwin* (New York: Oxford University Press, 2007), 8–11.

courses, although they might be of interest in courses on the history and philosophy of science. There is a problem, however. The claim that ID is bad science or dead science may depend, almost as much as the claim that it is not science, on the assumption that divine intervention in the natural order is not a serious possibility. That is not a scientific belief but a belief about a religious question: It amounts to the assumption that either there is no god or, if there is, he certainly does not intervene in the natural order to guide the world in certain directions.

The contrast between the rejection of ID and the rejection of creation science is instructive here. To reject the explanations creation scientists offer of the fossil record in terms of the biblical flood, we do not have to first assume that the Bible is not literally true. Even if we begin, for the sake of argument, with no prior assumptions about the literal truth of the Bible and assume that, prior to the geological evidence, it could be true, we will very quickly find overwhelming evidence that it is not—evidence that does not depend on ruling out in advance the possibility that the world was created six thousand years ago. All the conclusion depends on is not taking the literal truth of the Bible as an article of faith that cannot be refuted by any amount of contrary empirical evidence.

It is worth noting that this is a (negative) religious claim. To hold that empirical evidence can count against the literal truth of the Bible is to deny a religious belief that, remarkably, many people hold. That denial is a necessary condition of the teaching of much basic science. Since the Establishment Clause does not prohibit such teaching, it follows that there are certain religious beliefs whose implicit rejection in public education is not unconstitutional, precisely because they are inconsistent with the standards of scientific rationality.

Intelligent design is a different story. Its defense requires only that design be admitted as a possibility, not that it be regarded as empirically unassailable. It would be difficult to argue that the admission of that possibility is inconsistent with the standards of scientific rationality. Further, if it is admitted as a possibility, it would be difficult to argue that the currently available empirical evidence rules it out decisively, as it does young earth creationism. To rule it out decisively would require that the sufficiency of standard evolutionary mechanisms to account for the entire evolution of life should have been clearly established by the available evidence. So far as I can tell, in spite of rhetoric to the contrary, nothing close to this has been done.

A great deal depends on the likelihood that the complex chemical systems we observe arose through a sufficiently long sequence of random mutations in DNA, each of which enhanced fitness. It is difficult to find in the accessible literature the grounds for evolutionary biologists' confidence about this.[11] I am speaking as a layman, but it is to the lay public that the defense of scientific orthodoxy against ID is addressed. It is not enough to say, although it is true, that the *in*capacity of evolutionary mechanisms to account for the entire evolution of life has not been conclusively established. That is not required for an alternative to be considered seriously, provided the alternative is not ruled out in advance on other grounds. Those who offer empirical evidence for ID do not have to argue that a completely nonpurposive explanation is impossible, only that it is very unlikely, given the evidence available. That is a scientific claim, though a contestable one. The next step depends, as I have said, on beliefs about the possibility of design that are not based on that evidence, whether they are positive or negative.

[III]

The consequence of all this for public education is that both the inclusion of some mention of ID in a biology class and its exclusion would seem to depend on religious assumptions. Either divine intervention is ruled out in advance, or it is not. If it is, ID can be disregarded. If it is not, evidence for ID can be considered. Yet both are clearly assumptions of a religious nature. Public schools in the United States may not teach atheism or deism any more than they may teach Christianity, so how can it be all right to teach scientific theories whose empirical confirmation depends on the assumption of one range of these views while it is impermissible to discuss the implications of alternative views on the same question?

It would have to be argued that the assumption that divine intervention is impossible, or too improbable to be considered, is on a par with the assumption that the literal truth of the Bible is not immune to empirical counterevidence, and that just as the latter is a constitutionally permissible presupposition of the teaching of science, so is the former. In other words, not considering divine intervention a possibility is just a basic epistemological condition of modern science, a condition of scientific rationality, and cannot be constitutionally suspect, in spite of the fact that it is a religious assumption.

I know that many scientists would make this claim, and perhaps that is the nub of the issue. Yet it is inaccurate to assimilate the two religious positions

---

11. Confidence expressed by Jerry Coyne, for example, in his review of *The Edge of Evolution*: "Behe furnishes no proof, no convincing argument, that [protein-protein] interactions cannot evolve gradually. In fact, interactions between proteins, like any complex interaction, were certainly built up step by mutational step, with each change producing an interaction scrutinized by selection and retained if it enhanced an organism's fitness" (*The New Republic*, June 18, 2007, 42).

whose official exclusion is being said to be constitutionally required. In order to teach about the history of the universe, the solar system, and life on earth, it is indispensable to presuppose the falsity of fundamentalist epistemology. But the development of the theory of evolution did not depend on the assumption that design was impossible. On the contrary, it developed as an alternative to design, offering a surprising but illuminating account of how the appearance of design might have arisen without a designer. The conceivability of the design alternative is part of the background for understanding evolutionary theory. To make the assumption of its falsehood a condition of scientific rationality seems almost incoherent.

What would a biology course teach if it wanted to remain neutral on the question whether divine intervention in the process of life's development was a possibility, while acknowledging that people disagree about whether it should be regarded as a possibility at all, or what probability should be assigned to it, and that there is at present no way to settle that disagreement scientifically? So far as I can see, the only way to make no assumptions of a religious nature would be to admit that the empirical evidence may suggest different conclusions depending on what religious belief one starts with, and that the evidence does not by itself settle which of those beliefs is correct, even though there are other religious beliefs, such as the literal truth of Genesis, that are easily refuted by the evidence. I do not see much hope that such an approach could be adopted, but it would combine intellectual responsibility with respect for the Establishment Clause. Further (although the issue is not likely to arise), I believe that if a state legislature or school board voted to prohibit discussion of ID in the classroom, that would contravene the requirement of religious neutrality, although not as obviously as the exclusion of the theory of evolution, because it, too, would depend on a view, atheism or theistic noninterventionism, that falls clearly in the domain of religious belief.

Judge Jones cited as a decisive reason for denying ID the status of science that Michael Behe, the chief scientific witness for the defense, acknowledged that the theory would be more plausible to someone who believed in God than to someone who did not.[12] This is just common sense, however, and the opposite is just as true: Evolutionary theory as a complete explanation of the development of life is more plausible to someone who does not believe in God than to someone who does. Either both of them are science, or neither of them is. If

---

12. "Professor Behe remarkably and unmistakably claims that the *plausibility of the argument for ID depends upon the extent to which one believes in the existence of God.* As no evidence in the record indicates that any other scientific proposition's validity rests on belief in God, nor is the Court aware of any such scientific propositions, Professor Behe's assertion constitutes substantial evidence that in his view, as is commensurate with other prominent ID leaders, ID is a religious and not a scientific proposition" (*Kitzmiller*, at p. 720).

both of them are scientific hypotheses, the ground for exclusion must be that ID is hopelessly bad science, or dead science, in Kitcher's phrase.

That would be true if ID, like young earth creationism, can be refuted by the empirical evidence even if one starts by assuming that the possibility of a god who could intervene cannot be ruled out in advance. So far as I can tell, however, no such refutation has even been offered, let alone established. What have been offered instead are necessarily speculative proposals about how the problems posed by Behe might be handled by evolutionary theory, declarations that no hypothesis involving divine intervention counts as science, and assurances that evolutionary theory is not inconsistent with the existence of God. It is also emphasized that even if evolutionary theory were false, that would not mean that ID was true. That is so, but it is still not a sufficient reason to exclude it from discussion.

My own situation is that of an atheist who, in spite of being an avid consumer of popular science, has for a long time been skeptical of the claims of traditional evolutionary theory to be the whole story about the history of life. The theory does not claim to explain the origin of life, which remains a complete scientific mystery at this point. Opponents of ID, however, normally assume that that too must have a purely chemical explanation. The idea is that life arose and evolved to its present form solely because of the laws of chemistry, and ultimately of particle physics. In the prevailing naturalistic world view, evolutionary theory plays the crucial role in showing how physics can be the theory of everything.

Sophisticated members of the contemporary culture have been so thoroughly indoctrinated that they easily lose sight of the fact that evolutionary reductionism defies common sense. A theory that defies common sense can be true, but doubts about its truth should be suppressed only in the face of exceptionally strong evidence.

I do not regard divine intervention as a possibility, even though I have no other candidates. Yet I recognize that this is because of an aspect of my overall world view that does not rest on empirical grounds or any other kind of rational grounds. I do not think the existence of God can be disproved. So someone who can offer serious scientific reasons to doubt the adequacy of the theory of evolution, and who believes in God in the same immediate way that I believe there is no god, can quite reasonably conclude that the hypothesis of design should be taken seriously.[13] If reasons to doubt the adequacy of evolutionary

13. This presupposes the admittedly controversial position that reasonable people can disagree—so that I do not have to give up my belief that p even if I believe that others who believe not-p are not necessarily being irrational but are just mistaken.

theory can be legitimately admitted to the curriculum, it is hard to see why they cannot legitimately be described as reasons in support of design, for those who believe in God, and reasons to believe that some as yet undiscovered purely naturalistic theory must account for the evidence, for those who do not. That, after all, is the real epistemological situation.

Would it be an unconstitutional endorsement of religion to point this out in a biology course? It presumably would not have a prayer of acceptability if it were introduced at the behest of a school board whose religious members had adopted it as a fallback from something stronger. Suppose it were introduced by a more neutral school board, however, or by a biology teacher without noticeable religious beliefs, just in order to explain what is uncertain about evolutionary theory and what the possible responses are to that uncertainty.

What I think about this question owes a great deal to Kent Greenawalt's subtle and judicious book, *Does God Belong in Public Schools?*[14] written before the Dover decision but addressing many of the same issues. The Dover decision relied on two interpretations of the Establishment Clause: the *Lemon* test and the endorsement test. The *Lemon*[15] test requires that a law or practice must have a secular purpose, must not have a primary effect of either promoting or inhibiting religion, and must not foster excessive entanglement with religion. The endorsement test, enunciated by Justice O'Connor,[16] requires that the law or practice not have the purpose or effect of endorsing a particular religion or religion in general.

Interpretation of the Establishment Clause is unsettled and evolving, but if we take these two tests as a guide, the mention of ID seems constitutionally defensible. If properly presented, it could be defended as having the secular purpose of providing a better understanding of evolutionary theory and of the evidence for and against it. Would it fail on the ground that one of its principal effects would be to advance religion?

It has to be admitted that, by suggesting that the existence of God is a possibility and that if there is a god he might have played a role in the development of life, it would have such an effect. That might be too much religion by current standards. By the same token, such teaching would also advance atheism, by suggesting that the nonexistence of God was a serious possibility, so it might lose from both directions. Perhaps silence on the subject of the relation between evolutionary theory and religious belief is the only course compatible with the Establishment Clause.

---

14. Kent Greenawalt, *Does God Belong in Public Schools?* (Princeton, N.J.: Princeton University Press, 2005).

15. *Lemon v. Kurtzman*, 403 US 602 (1971).

16. In *Wallace v. Jaffree*, 472 US 38 (1985).

It would be a shame if this were so. Greenawalt, after discussing the issue with great care, concludes that a very limited opening of the topic is warranted:

> [S]cience teachers should cover the evidential gaps and controversies surrounding the neo-Darwinian synthesis. Any evidence for a kind of order of a sort not yet integrated into the dominant theory should be fairly presented. Teachers should indicate that present uncertainties by no means show that the dominant theory is incapable of explaining everything important. They should also explain that if the development of life has proceeded partly on the basis of an order that present neo-Darwinian theory neglects, that order may or may not reflect an intelligent designer; but that modern science has discovered naturally explicable principles of order for much that once seemed beyond explaining. Science teachers should *not* get far into the question of whether any as yet undiscovered principles of order in evolution, were they to exist, are likely to have proceeded from creative intelligence. One reason not to engage this possibility at any length is that students with religious objections to standard evolutionary theory may build much more than is warranted from any scientific perspective from conjectures about intelligent design.[17]

Even something this cautious would probably be unacceptable to the scientific establishment, but I would like to believe that something less inhibited would be admissible, namely, a frank discussion of the relation of evolutionary theory to religion in some part of the high school curriculum. If biology teachers would be too burdened by this task, room should be found for it elsewhere.

I think the true position of those who would exclude intelligent design from the domain of science is that things have changed fundamentally since 1859. In other words, when Darwin published *The Origin of Species* it may have been appropriate to present it as an alternative to design, just as Copernicus had to present the heliocentric theory as an alternative to the geocentric theory. Yet now, after all that has happened over the past century and a half, the very idea of design is as dead as Ptolemaic astronomy: A reductive and above all purposeless naturalism can be taken for granted as the only possible form of explanation in biology. To exclude the possibility of divine intervention in the history of life is scientifically legitimate, and to assign it any antecedent positive probability at all is irrational. To the extent that such a prior probability affects

---

17. Greenawalt, *Does God Belong in Public Schools?* 115.

conclusions drawn from the evidence, they too are irrational and cannot be taken seriously as scientific proposals.

Judge Jones is careful to say, "We express no opinion on the ultimate veracity of ID as a supernatural explanation."[18] This is not the position of most evolutionary scientists, however. They believe that there are no supernatural explanations, and that trying to show that they are incompatible with the evidence is a waste of time. It is part of their basic epistemological and metaphysical framework, which either excludes the existence of God or, at best, places him entirely outside the boundaries of the natural universe. They do not think, "Maybe there are supernatural explanations, but if there are, science cannot discover them." Rather, they think, "Anybody who is willing even to consider supernatural explanations is living in the past."

But we can't make this a fundamental principle of public education. I understand the attitude that ID is just the latest manifestation of the fundamentalist threat, and that you have to stand and fight them here or you will end up having to fight for the right to teach evolution at all. However, I believe that both intellectually and constitutionally the line doesn't have to be drawn at this point, and that a noncommittal discussion of some of the issues would be preferable.

---

18. *Kitzmiller*, at p. 746.

PART II

Politics

6

The Problem of Global Justice

[I]

We do not live in a just world. This may be the least controversial claim one could make in political theory. But it is much less clear what, if anything, justice on a world scale might mean, or what the hope for justice should lead us to want in the domain of international or global institutions and in the policies of states that are in a position to affect the world order.

By comparison with the perplexing and undeveloped state of this subject, domestic political theory is very well understood, with multiple highly developed theories offering alternative solutions to well-defined problems. By contrast, concepts and theories of global justice are in the early stages of formation, and it is not clear what the main questions are, let alone the main possible answers. I believe that the need for workable ideas about the global or international case presents political theory with its most important current task, and even perhaps with the opportunity to make a practical contribution in the long run—though perhaps only the very long run.

The theoretical and normative questions I want to discuss are closely related to pressing practical questions that we now face about the legitimate path forward in the governance of the world. These are, inevitably, questions about institutions, many of which do not yet exist. However imperfectly, the nation-state is the primary locus of political legitimacy and the pursuit of justice, and it is one of the advantages of domestic political theory that nation-states actually exist. But when we are presented with the need for collective action on a global scale, it is very unclear what, if anything, could play a comparable role.

The concept of justice can be used in evaluating many different things, from the criminal law to the market economy. In a broad sense of the term, the international requirements of justice include standards governing the justification and conduct of war and standards that define the most basic human rights. Some standards of these two kinds have achieved a measure of international recognition over the past half century. They define certain types of criminal conduct, usually by states, against other states or against individuals or ethnic groups. But this is not the aspect of global justice that I will concentrate on. My concern here is not with war crimes or crimes against humanity but with socioeconomic justice, and whether anything can be made of it on a world scale.

I will approach the question by focusing on the application to the world as a whole of two central issues of traditional political theory: the relation between justice and sovereignty, and the scope and limits of equality as a demand of justice. The two issues are related, and both are of crucial importance in determining whether we can even form an intelligible ideal of global justice.

The issue of justice and sovereignty was memorably formulated by Hobbes. He argued that though we can discover true principles of justice by moral reasoning alone, actual justice cannot be achieved except within a sovereign state. Justice as a property of the relations among human beings (and also injustice, for the most part) requires government as an enabling condition. Hobbes drew the obvious consequence for the international arena, where he saw separate sovereigns inevitably facing each other in a state of war, from which both justice and injustice are absent.

The issue of justice and equality is posed with particular clarity by one of the controversies between Rawls and his critics. Rawls argued that the liberal requirements of justice include a strong component of equality among citizens, but that this is a specifically political demand, which applies to the basic structure of a unified nation-state. It does not apply to the personal (nonpolitical) choices of individuals living in such a society, nor does it apply to the relations between one society and another or between the members of different societies. Egalitarian justice is a requirement on the internal political, economic, and social structure of nation-states and cannot be extrapolated to different contexts, which require different standards. This issue is independent of the specific standards of egalitarian justice found in Rawls's theory. Whatever standards of equal rights or equal opportunity apply domestically, the question is whether consistency requires that they also apply globally.

If Hobbes is right, the idea of global justice without a world government is a chimera. If Rawls is right, perhaps there can be something that might be called justice or injustice in the relations between states, but it bears only a distant relation to the evaluation of societies themselves as just or unjust: For the most part, the ideal of a just world for Rawls would have to be the ideal of a world of internally just states living at peace with one another.

[II]

It seems to me difficult not to accept some version of Hobbes's claim about the relation between justice and sovereignty. There is much more to his political theory than this, of course. Among other things, he based political legitimacy and the principles of justice on collective self-interest, rather than on any irreducibly moral premises. And he defended absolute monarchy as the best form of sovereignty. But the relation between justice and sovereignty is a separable question, and Hobbes's position can be defended in connection with theories of justice and moral evaluation very different from his.

What creates the link between justice and sovereignty is something common to a wide range of conceptions of justice: They all depend on the coordinated conduct of large numbers of people, which cannot be achieved without law backed up by a monopoly of force. Hobbes construed the principles of justice, and more broadly the moral law, as a set of rules and practices that would serve everyone's interest if everyone conformed to them. This collective self-interest cannot be realized by the independent motivation of self-interested individuals unless each of them has the assurance that others will conform if he does. That assurance requires the external incentive provided by the sovereign, who sees to it that individual and collective self-interest coincide. At least among sizable populations, it cannot be provided by voluntary conventions supported solely by the mutual recognition of a common interest.

But the same need for assurance is present if one construes the principles of justice differently and attributes to individuals a non-self-interested motive that leads them to want to live on fair terms of some kind with other people. Even if justice is taken to include not only collective self-interest but also the elimination of morally arbitrary inequalities, or the protection of rights to liberty, the existence of a just order still depends on consistent patterns of conduct and persisting institutions that have a pervasive effect on the shape of people's lives. Separate individuals, however attached to such an ideal, have no motive, or even opportunity, to conform to such patterns or institutions on their own, without the assurance that their conduct will in fact be part of a reliable and effective system.

The only way to provide that assurance is through some form of law, with centralized authority to determine the rules and a centralized monopoly of the power of enforcement. This is needed even in a community most of whose members are attached to a common ideal of justice, both in order to provide terms of coordination and because it doesn't take many defectors to make such a system unravel. The kind of all-encompassing collective practice or institution that is capable of being just in the primary sense can exist only under sovereign authority. It is only the operation of such a system that one can judge to be just or unjust.

According to Hobbes, in the absence of the enabling condition of sovereign power, individuals are famously thrown back on their own resources and led by the legitimate motive of self-preservation to a defensive, distrustful posture of war. They hope for the conditions of peace and justice and support their creation whenever it seems safe to do so, but they cannot pursue justice by themselves.

I believe that the situation is structurally not very different for conceptions of justice that are based on much more other-regarding motives. Without the enabling condition of sovereignty to confer stability on just institutions, individuals, however morally motivated, can only fall back on a pure aspiration for justice that has no practical expression, apart from the willingness to support just institutions, should they become possible.

The other-regarding motives that support adherence to just institutions when they exist do not provide clear guidance where the enabling conditions for such institutions do not exist, as seems to be true for the world as a whole. Those motives, even if they make us dissatisfied with our relations to other human beings, are baffled and left without an avenue of expression, except for the expression of moral frustration.

[III]

Hobbes himself was not disturbed by the appearance of this problem in the international case, since he believed that the essential aim of justice, collective security and self-interest, could be effectively provided for individuals through the sovereignty of separate states. In a famous passage, he says:

> [I]n all times, kings, and persons of sovereign authority, because
> of their independency, are in continual jealousies, and in the state

and posture of gladiators; having their weapons pointing, and their eyes fixed on one another; that is, their forts, garrisons, and guns upon the frontiers of their kingdoms; and continual spies upon their neighbours; which is a posture of war. But because they uphold thereby, the industry of their subjects; there does not follow from it, that misery, which accompanies the liberty of particular men.[1]

The absence of sovereignty over the globe, in other words, is not a serious obstacle to justice in the relations among the citizens of each sovereign state, and that is what matters.

This position is more problematic for those who do not share Hobbes's belief that the foundation of justice is collective self-interest and that the attachment of any individual to just institutions is based solely on his own good. If Hobbes were right, a person's interest in justice would be served provided he himself lived in a stable society governed in accordance with the rules of peace, security, and economic order. But for most of us, the ideal of justice stems from moral motives that cannot be entirely reduced to self-interest.

It includes much more than a condition of legally enforced peace and security among interacting individuals, together with stable property rights and the reliability of contracts. Most modern conceptions of justice impose some limits on the powers of sovereignty—in the name of non-Hobbesian individual rights to liberty—and some condition of fairness or equality in the way the institutions of a just society treat its citizens, not only politically but economically and socially. It is this last element that creates unease over the complete absence of any comparable standards of fairness or equality of opportunity from the practices that govern our relations with individuals in other societies.

The gruesome facts of inequality in the world economy are familiar. Though the situation has improved greatly over the past twenty-five years, especially in Asia, roughly 20 percent of the world's population live on less than $1.25 a day, according to the World Bank, whereas the 15 percent who live in the high-income economies have an average per capita income of $75 a day. How are we to respond to such facts?

There is a peculiar problem here for our discussion: The facts are so grim that justice may be a side issue. Whatever view one takes of the applicability or inapplicability of standards of justice to such a situation, it is clearly a disaster from a more broadly humanitarian point of view. I assume there is some minimal concern we owe to fellow human beings threatened with starvation or severe malnutrition and early death from easily preventable diseases, as all

---

1. Thomas Hobbes, *Leviathan*, chap. 13.

these people in dire poverty are. Although there is plenty of room for disagreement about the most effective methods, some form of humane assistance from the well off to those in extremis is clearly called for quite apart from any demand of justice, if we are not simply ethical egoists. The urgent current issue, more basic than global justice, is what can be done in the world economy to reduce extreme global poverty. These basic duties of humanity also present serious problems of what we should do individually and collectively to fulfill them in the absence of global sovereignty, and in spite of the obstacles often presented by malfunctioning state sovereignty. But I am posing a different question, one that is morally less urgent but philosophically harder.

Justice as ordinarily understood requires more than mere humanitarian assistance to those in desperate need, and injustice can exist without anyone being on the verge of starvation. Humanitarian duties hold in virtue of the absolute rather than the relative level of need of the people we are in a position to help. Justice, by contrast, is concerned with the relations between the conditions of different classes of people and the causes of inequality between them. My question is about how to respond to world inequality in general from the point of view of justice and injustice rather than humanity alone. The answer to that question will depend crucially on one's moral conception of the relation between the value of justice and the existence of the institutions that sovereign authority makes possible. There are two principal conceptions that I want to consider.

According to the first conception, which is usually called *cosmopolitanism*, the demands of justice derive from an equal concern or a duty of fairness that we owe in principle to all our fellow human beings, and the institutions to which standards of justice can be applied are instruments for the fulfillment of that duty. Such instruments are in fact only selectively available: We may be able to live on just terms only with those others who are fellow members of sufficiently robust and well-ordered sovereign states. But the moral basis for the requirements of justice that should govern those states is universal in scope—it is a concern for the fairness of the terms on which we share the world with anyone.[2]

---

2. See Peter Singer, *One World* (New Haven, Conn.: Yale University Press, 2002); Thomas Pogge, *Realizing Rawls* (Ithaca, N.Y.: Cornell University Press, 1989), 240–80; Thomas Pogge, *World Poverty and Human Rights* (Cambridge: Polity Press, 2002); and Charles Beitz, *Political Theory and International Relations* (Princeton, N.J.: Princeton University Press, 1979). I am leaving aside here the very important differences over what the universal foundation of cosmopolitan justice is. Cosmopolitans can be utilitarians, liberal egalitarians, or even libertarian defenders of laissez faire, provided they think these moral standards of equal treatment apply in principle to our relations to all other persons, not just to our fellow citizens.

If one takes the cosmopolitan view, the existence of separate sovereign states is an unfortunate obstacle, though perhaps for the foreseeable future an insurmountable one, to the establishment or even the pursuit of global justice. But it would be morally inconsistent not to wish, for the world as a whole, a common system of institutions that could attempt to realize the same standards of fairness or equal opportunity that one wants for one's own society. The accident of being born in a poor rather than a rich country is as arbitrary a determinant of one's fate as the accident of being born into a poor rather than a rich family in the same country. In the absence of global sovereignty we may not, for Hobbesian reasons, be able to describe the world economic order as *un*just, but the absence of justice is a defect all the same.

Cosmopolitan justice could be realized in a federal system, in which the members of individual nation-states had special responsibilities toward one another that they did not have for everyone in the world. But that would be legitimate only against the background of a global system that prevented such special responsibilities from generating injustice on a larger scale. This would be analogous to the requirement that within a state, the institutions of private property, which allow people to pursue their private ends without constantly taking into account the aims of justice, should nevertheless be arranged so that societal injustice is not their indirect consequence.[3]

Unlike cosmopolitanism, the second conception of justice does not have a standard name, but let me call it the *political* conception, since it is exemplified by Rawls's view that justice should be understood as a specifically political value, rather than being derived from a comprehensive moral system, so that it is essentially a virtue—the first virtue—of social institutions.

On the political conception, sovereign states are not merely instruments for realizing the preinstitutional value of justice among human beings. Instead, their existence is precisely what gives the value of justice its application, by putting the fellow citizens of a sovereign state into a relation that they do not have with the rest of humanity—an institutional relation which must then be evaluated by the special standards of fairness and equality that fill out the content of justice.

Another representative of the political conception is Ronald Dworkin, who expresses it this way:

---

3. A subtle version of such a system has been outlined by Janos Kis in "The Unity of Mankind and the Plurality of States" (unpublished manuscript). He calls it a *supranation-state regime*: Separate states would retain primary responsibility for just governance but share sovereign power with international institutions with special authority defined functionally and not territorially—with respect to trade, the environment, human rights, and the like. See section VIII below for some questions about applying cosmopolitan norms at this level.

> A political community that exercises dominion over its own citizens, and demands from them allegiance and obedience to its laws, must take up an impartial, objective attitude toward them all, and each of its citizens must vote, and its officials must enact laws and form governmental policies, with that responsibility in mind. Equal concern...is the special and indispensable virtue of sovereigns.[4]

Every state has the boundaries and population it has for all sorts of accidental and historical reasons, but given that it exercises sovereign power over its citizens and in their name, those citizens have a duty of justice toward one another through the legal, social, and economic institutions that sovereign power makes possible. This duty is *sui generis*, and is not owed to everyone in the world, nor is it an indirect consequence of any other duty that may be owed to everyone in the world, such as a duty of humanity. Justice is something we owe through our shared institutions only to those with whom we stand in a strong political relation. It is, in the standard terminology, an *associative* obligation.

Furthermore, though the obligations of justice arise as a result of a special relation, there is no obligation to enter into that relation with those to whom we do not yet have it, thereby acquiring those obligations toward them. If we find ourselves in such a relation, then we must accept the obligations, but we do not have to seek them out, and may even try to avoid incurring them—as with other contingent obligations of a more personal kind: One doesn't have to marry and have children, for example.

If one takes this political view, one will not find the absence of global justice a cause for distress. There is a lot else to be distressed about: world misery, for example, and also the egregious internal injustice of so many of the world's sovereign states. Someone who accepts the political conception of justice may even hold that there is a secondary duty to promote just institutions for societies that do not have them. But the requirements of justice themselves do not, on this view, apply to the world as a whole, unless and until, as a result of historical developments not required by justice, the world comes to be governed by a unified sovereign power.

The political conception of justice therefore arrives, by a different route, at the same conclusion as Hobbes: The full standards of justice, though they can be known by moral reasoning, apply only within the boundaries of a sovereign state, however arbitrary those boundaries may be. Internationally, there may well be standards of right and wrong, but they do not merit the full name of justice.

---

4. Ronald Dworkin, *Sovereign Virtue* (Cambridge, Mass.: Harvard University Press, 2000), 6.

[IV]

On either the cosmopolitan or the political view, global justice would require global sovereignty. But there is still a huge difference between the two views in the attitude they take toward this conclusion. On the political view, the absence of global justice need not be a matter of regret; on the cosmopolitan view, it is, and the obstacles to global sovereignty pose a serious moral problem. Let me now consider the issue of principle between the two conceptions. While we should keep in mind that different views about the content of justice can be combined with either of these two conceptions of its scope, I'll continue to use Rawls to exemplify the political view. But most of what I will say is independent of the main disagreements over the content of domestic justice—political, economic, or social.

Rawls's political conception of justice is an example of a more general feature of his approach to moral theory—his rejection of what Liam Murphy calls *monism*. Murphy has introduced this term to designate the idea that "any plausible overall political/moral view must, at the fundamental level, evaluate the justice of institutions with normative principles that apply also to people's choices." The opposite view, which Murphy calls *dualism*, is that "the two practical problems of institutional design and personal conduct require, at the fundamental level, two different kinds of practical principle."[5] (The term "dualism" is not ideal for the contrast, since, as we shall see, there are more than two levels at which independent moral principles may apply.)

Rawls is famous for insisting that different principles apply to different types of entities: that "the correct regulative principle for a thing depends on the nature of that thing."[6] The most noted instance of this is his argument against utilitarianism, which he criticizes for applying to a society of individuals the principles of aggregating and maximizing net benefits minus costs that are appropriate within the life of a single individual, but inappropriate for groups of individuals. "Utilitarianism," he says, "does not take seriously the distinction between persons."[7]

But the point applies more widely. Rawls's antimonism is essential to understanding both his domestic theory of a just society and his view of the relation between domestic and international principles, as expressed in *The*

---

5. Liam Murphy, "Institutions and the Demands of Justice," *Philosophy and Public Affairs* 27 (1998), 253–54.

6. John Rawls, *A Theory of Justice*, revised edition (Cambridge, Mass.: Harvard University Press, 1999), 25.

7. Rawls, *A Theory of Justice*, 24.

Law of Peoples. His two principles of justice are designed to regulate neither the personal conduct of individuals living in a just society, nor the governance of private associations, nor the international relations of societies to one another, but only the basic structure of separate nation-states. It is the nature of sovereign states, he believes, and in particular their comprehensive control over the framework of their citizens' lives, that creates the special demands for justification and the special constraints on ends and means that constitute the requirements of justice.

In Rawls's domestic theory, this expresses itself in two ways: first, in the priority of individual liberty, which leaves people free to pursue their own personal ends rather than requiring them to pursue just outcomes privately; and, second, in the application of the difference principle not to the distribution of advantages and disadvantages to individuals, but rather to the probabilistic distribution of ex ante life prospects (which always include a range) to those born into different socioeconomic classes. Even if the basic structure supported by law satisfies the difference principle by arranging inequalities to maximize the expectations of the lowest class in this sense, individual choices are not expected to be governed by that principle. Those choices will result in substantial inequalities in actual outcomes among individuals within each socioeconomic class, in addition to the inequalities in ex ante life prospects between classes permitted by the difference principle itself.

So Rawls's egalitarianism doesn't apply either to individual morality or to individual outcomes within the bounds of an egalitarian state. But neither does it apply to the relations between states, nor between the individual members of different states. These are all different cases or types of relation, and the principles that govern them have to be arrived at separately. They cannot be reached by extending to the international case the principles of domestic justice.

Internationally, Rawls finds the main expression of moral constraints not in a relation among individuals but in a limited requirement of mutual respect and equality of status among peoples. This is more constraining than the traditional Hobbesian privileges of sovereignty on the world stage; it is a substantial moral order, far from the state of nature. But the moral units of the order are peoples, not individuals, and the values have to do with the relations among these collective units rather than the relations of individuals across the world.

Just as, within a state, what we owe one another as fellow citizens through our common institutions is very different from what we owe one another as private individuals, so internationally, what we owe to other inhabitants of the globe through our society's respect for the societies of which they are citizens is different both from what we owe to our fellow citizens and from what we as individuals owe to all our fellow human beings. The duties governing the relations among peoples include, according to Rawls, not only nonaggression and fidelity to treaties but also some developmental assistance to "peoples living under unfavorable conditions that prevent their having a just or decent political and social regime."[8] But they do not include any analogue of liberal socioeconomic justice.

This limitation is rejected by cosmopolitan critics of Rawls. The issue is the choice of moral units. The monist idea is that the basic constituency for all morality must be individuals, not societies or peoples, and that whatever moral requirements apply either to social institutions or to international relations must ultimately be justified by their effects on individuals—and by a morality that governs the treatment of all individuals by all other individuals.

From this point of view it seems natural to conclude that any such morality must count all individual lives as equally valuable or important, and that in particular it must not allow international boundaries to count at the most basic level in determining how one individual should take into consideration the interests of another. The consequence seems to be that if one wants to avoid moral inconsistency, and is sympathetic to Rawls's theory of justice, one should favor a global difference principle, perhaps backed up by a global original position in which all individuals are represented behind the veil of ignorance.[9]

But whatever we think about the original position, Rawls must resist the charge that moral consistency requires him to take individuals as the moral units in a conception of global justice. To do so would make a huge difference, for it would mean that applying the principles of justice within the bounds of the nation-state was at best a practical stopgap.

Rawls's antimonism is in essence a theoretical rejection of such standards for moral consistency. In his view, just as there is no inconsistency in governing interpersonal relations by principles very different from those that govern legal institutions, so there need be no inconsistency in governing the world differently from its political subdivisions. But if what we are looking for is moral,

---

8. John Rawls, *The Law of Peoples* (Cambridge, Mass.: Harvard University Press, 1999), 37.

9. Rawls himself proposes a "second original position," with representatives of peoples as the parties behind the veil of ignorance—but he doesn't really try to arrive at principles on that basis (*The Law of Peoples*, 32–42). I should mention that Rawls's *original* original position, the attempt to model a moral choice for handling conflicts of interest among distinct parties by the device of an individual choice under radical uncertainty about which of the parties one is, seems to me to violate Rawls's own insistence that different principles are appropriate for answering different kinds of questions. The original position might even be charged with failing to take seriously the distinction between persons, since no individual choice, even a choice under uncertainty, is equivalent to a choice for a group. This is confirmed by the difficulty Rawls has in showing that his principles of justice would be chosen by individuals in the original position. For example, he has to exclude any assignment of probabilities to their belonging to one social class rather than another, an exclusion that seems arbitrary when we think of the original position purely as a self-regarding choice under uncertainty.

and not just logical, consistency, the differences between the cases must in some way explain why different principles are appropriate.

The way to resist cosmopolitanism fundamentally would be to deny that there is a universal pressure toward equal concern, equal status, and equal opportunity. One could admit a universal humanitarian requirement of minimal concern (which, even in the world as it is, would not be terribly onerous, provided all the prosperous countries did their share). But the defense of the political conception of justice would have to hold that beyond the basic humanitarian duties, further requirements of equal treatment depend on a strong condition of associative responsibility, that such responsibility is created by specific and contingent relations such as fellow citizenship, and that there is no general moral requirement to take responsibility for others by getting into those sorts of relations with as many of them as possible.

This would still count as a universal principle, but it would imply a strongly differentiated system of moral obligations. If the conditions of even the poorest societies should come to meet a livable minimum, the political conception might not even see a general humanitarian claim for redistribution. This makes it a very convenient view for those living in rich societies to hold. But that alone doesn't make it false.

[V]

I find the choice between these two incompatible moral conceptions difficult. The cosmopolitan conception has considerable moral appeal, because it seems highly arbitrary that the average individual born into a poor society should have radically lower life prospects than the average individual born into a rich one, just as arbitrary as the corresponding difference between rich and poor in a rich but unjust society. The cosmopolitan conception points us toward the utopian goal of trying to extend legitimate democratic governance to ever larger domains in pursuit of more global justice.

But I will not explore that possibility further. Without trying to refute cosmopolitanism I will instead pursue a fuller account of the grounds and content of the political conception. I am going to follow this fork in the path partly because I believe the political conception is accepted by most people in the privileged nations of the world, so that, true or false, it will have a significant role in determining what happens. I also think it is probably correct.

Let me try to spell out the kind of political conception that seems to me plausible. Even though I am skeptical about grounding it in a hypothetical contract of the type Rawls proposes, its debt to the social contract tradition will be obvious.[10]

We can begin by noting that even on the political conception, some conditions of justice don't depend on associative obligations. The protection, under sovereign power, of negative rights like bodily inviolability, freedom of expression, and freedom of religion is morally unmysterious. Those rights, if they exist, set universal and prepolitical limits to the legitimate use of power, independent of special forms of association. It is wrong for any individual or group to deny such rights to any other individual or group, and we do not give them up as a condition of membership in a political society—even though their precise boundaries and methods of protection through law will have to be determined politically in light of each society's particular circumstances.

Socioeconomic justice is different. On the political conception it is fully associative. It depends on positive rights that we do not have against all other persons or groups, rights that arise only because we are joined together with certain others in a political society under strong centralized control. It is only from such a system, and from our fellow members through its institutions, that we can claim a right to democracy, equal citizenship, nondiscrimination, equality of opportunity, and the amelioration through public policy of unfairness in the distribution of social and economic goods.

In presenting the intuitive moral case for the particular principles of justice he favors as the embodiment of these ideals, Rawls appeals repeatedly to the importance of eliminating or reducing morally arbitrary sources of inequality in people's life prospects.[11] He means inequalities flowing from characteristics of people that they have done nothing to deserve, like their race, their sex, the wealth or poverty of their parents, and their inborn natural endowments. To the extent that such factors, through the operation of a particular social system, generate differences in people's expectations, at birth, of better or worse lives, they present a problem for the justification of that system. In some respects these arbitrary sources of inequality can be eliminated, but Rawls holds that where they remain, some other justification needs to be found for permitting them.

The important point for our purposes is that Rawls believes that this moral presumption against arbitrary inequalities is not a principle of universal

10. In "Distributive Justice, State Coercion, and Autonomy," *Philosophy and Public Affairs* 30 (2001), 257–96, Michael Blake defends very similar moral conclusions—specifically that although absolute deprivation is an international concern, relative deprivation is not. But he bases his argument on the rather different ground of autonomy and what is needed to justify coercion.

11. See Rawls, *A Theory of Justice*, chap. II, and Rawls, *Justice as Fairness: A Restatement* (Cambridge, Mass.: Harvard University Press, 2001), part II.

application. It might have considerable appeal if recast as a universal principle, to the effect that there is something prima facie objectionable to anyone's having lower life prospects at birth than anyone else just because of a difference between the two of them, such as the wealth of their parents or their nationality, over which neither of them had any control. But this is not the principle Rawls is appealing to. Rather, in his theory the objection to arbitrary inequalities gets a foothold only because of the societal context. What is objectionable is that we should be fellow participants in a collective enterprise of coercively imposed legal and political institutions that generates such arbitrary inequalities.

What is interesting and somewhat surprising about this condition is that such comembership is itself arbitrary, so an arbitrary distinction is responsible for the scope of the presumption against arbitrariness. We do not deserve to have been born into a particular society any more than we deserve to have been born into a particular family. Those who are not immigrants have done nothing to become members of their society. The egalitarian requirement is based not on actual choice, consent, or contract, but on involuntary membership. It is only the internal character of the system in which we arbitrarily find ourselves that gives rise to the special presumption against further arbitrary distinctions within it.

Since there are equally arbitrary extrasocietal distinctions that do not carry the same moral weight, the ground for the presumption cannot be merely that these intrasocietal inequalities have a profound effect on people's lives. The fact that they shape people's life prospects from birth is necessary but not sufficient to explain the presumption against them. So what is the additional necessary condition?

I believe it comes from a special involvement of agency or the will that is inseparable from membership in a political society. Not the will to become or remain a member, for most people have no choice in that regard, but the engagement of the will that is essential to life inside a society, in the dual role each member plays both as one of the society's subjects and as one of those in whose name its authority is exercised. One might even say that we are all participants in the general will. It is in this sense that Rawls's theory belongs to the social contract tradition.

A sovereign state is not just a cooperative enterprise for mutual advantage. The societal rules determining its basic structure are coercively imposed: It is not a voluntary association. I submit that it is this complex fact—that we are both putative joint authors of the coercively imposed system, and subject to its norms, that is, expected to accept their authority even when the collective decision diverges from our personal preferences—that creates the special presumption against arbitrary inequalities in our treatment by the system.

Without being given a choice, we are assigned a role in the collective life of a particular society. The society makes us responsible for its acts, which are taken in our name and on which, in a democracy, we may even have some influence, and it holds us responsible for obeying its laws and conforming to its norms, thereby supporting the institutions through which advantages and disadvantages are created and distributed.[12] Insofar as those institutions admit arbitrary inequalities, we are, even though the responsibility has been simply handed to us, responsible for them—and we therefore have standing to ask why we should accept them. This request for justification has moral weight even if we have in practice no choice but to live under the existing regime. The reason is that its requirements claim our active cooperation, and this cannot be legitimately done without justification—otherwise it is pure coercion.[13]

The required active engagement of the will of each member of the society in its operation is crucial. It is not enough to appeal to the large material effects that the system imposes on its members. The immigration policies of one country may impose large effects on the lives of those living in other countries, but under the political conception, that by itself does not imply that such policies should be determined in a way that gives the interests and opportunities of those others equal consideration. Immigration policies are simply enforced against the nationals of other states; the laws are not imposed in their name, nor are they asked to accept and uphold those laws. Since no acceptance is demanded of them, no justification is required that explains why they should accept such discriminatory policies, or why their interests have been given equal consideration. It is sufficient justification to claim that the policies do not violate their prepolitical human rights.

That doesn't mean that on the political conception one state may do anything whatever to the citizens of another. States are entitled to be left to their own devices, but only on the condition that they not harm others. Even

---

12. Janos Kis has pointed out to me that there is also a significant negative aspect to our collective responsibility for one another. If our society has inflicted wrongs that demand compensation, we are obliged to contribute to those reparations, whether we individually played a part in the wrongs or not. So there is more than one way in which—to use a phrase of Rawls—the members of a society "share one another's fate."

13. I have stated these conditions of justice in a way that applies to self-governing societies. Robert Post has put to me the excellent question whether on the political conception justice is owed to the subjects of regimes that are imposed from outside, such as colonial regimes or regimes of military occupation (such as those imposed on Germany and Japan after World War II). Even if we set aside the issue of whether colonial rule is ipso facto unjust, I believe the answer to Post's question is yes. Does this require a modification of my conditions? I believe it requires a broad interpretation of what it is for a society to be governed in the name of its members. But I think it can be said that if a colonial or occupying power claims political authority over a population, it purports not to rule by force alone. It is providing and enforcing a system of law that those subject to it are expected to uphold as participants, and that is intended to serve their interests even if they are not its legislators. Since their normative engagement is required, there is a sense in which it is being imposed in their name.

a nation's immunity from the need to justify to outsiders the limits on access to its territory is not absolute. In extreme circumstances, denial of the right of immigration may constitute a failure to respect human rights or the universal duty of rescue. This is recognized in special provisions for political asylum, for example. The most basic rights and duties are universal, and not contingent on specific institutional relations between people. Only the heightened requirements of equal treatment embodied in principles of justice, including political equality, equality of opportunity, and distributive justice, are contingent in this way.

To be sure, even within a state, through economic competition, for example, some members or associations of members may impose serious consequences on others without any implication that the others are asked to accept or authorize the actions that have those consequences. Citizens are not expected to treat each other equally in private transactions. But the broader legal framework that makes those actions possible and legally sustains their results is subject to collective authority and justification and therefore to principles of social justice: not act by act, but for the system as a whole.

In short, the state makes unique demands on the will of its members—or the members make unique demands on one another through the institutions of the state—and those exceptional demands bring with them exceptional obligations, the positive obligations of justice. Those obligations reach no further than the demands do, and that explains the special character of the political conception.

[VI]

What is the overall moral outlook that best fits the political conception of justice? Although it is based on a rejection of monism and does not derive its content from a universal moral relation in which we stand to all persons, the political conception does not deny that there is such a relation. Political institutions create contingent, selective moral relations, but there are also noncontingent, universal relations in which we stand to everyone, and political justice is surrounded by this larger moral context.

The normative force of the most basic human rights against violence, enslavement, and coercion, and of the most basic humanitarian duties of rescue from immediate danger, depends only on our capacity to put ourselves in other people's shoes. The interests protected by such moral requirements are so fundamental, and the burdens they impose, considered statistically, so much slighter, that a criterion of universalizability of the Kantian type clearly

supports them. I say "statistically" because the restrictions implied by individual rights can in particular cases be very demanding: You may not kill an
innocent person to save your life, for example. But the importance to all of us of
blanket immunity from such violation dominates the slight danger that we will
be called on to lose our lives rather than violate the constraint. This is based not
on a utilitarian calculation but on the great importance to each person of the
kind of inviolability conferred by rights. Rights are a guarantee to each of us of
a certain protected status, rather than a net benefit to the aggregate.

This minimal humanitarian morality governs our relation to all other persons. It does not require us to make their ends our own, but it does require us
to pursue our ends within boundaries that leave them free to pursue theirs, and
to relieve them from extreme threats and obstacles to such freedom if we can do
so without serious sacrifice of our own ends. I take this to be the consequence
of the type of contractualist standard expressed by Kant's categorical imperative
and developed in one version by Scanlon.[14] To specify it any less vaguely would
require a full moral theory, which I will not attempt even to sketch here.

This moral minimum does not depend on the existence of any institutional connection between ourselves and other persons: It governs our relations
with everyone in the world. However, it may be impossible to fulfill even our
minimal moral duties to others without the help of institutions of some kind
short of sovereignty. We do not need institutions to enable us to refrain from
violating other people's rights, but institutions are indispensable to enable us
to fulfill the duty of rescue toward people in dire straits all over the world. Further, it seems clear that human rights generate a secondary obligation to do
something, if we can, to protect people outside of our society against their most
egregious violation, and this is practically impossible, on a world scale, without
some institutionalized methods of verification and enforcement.

The first of these roles, that of rescue, can be filled to some extent by non-
governmental organizations (NGOs) that operate internationally but privately,
providing individuals with the opportunity to contribute to relief of famine and
disease. Even the second role, protection of rights, has its private institutional
actors in the form of organizations like Amnesty International and Human
Rights Watch. But successful action on a much larger scale would be possible through international institutions supported by governments, both with
funds and with enforcement. The World Bank is in some respects such an
institution, and the International Criminal Court aspires to be. The question is
whether international developments will countenance the bending of national

14. T. M. Scanlon, *What We Owe to Each Other* (Cambridge, Mass.: Harvard University Press, 1998).

sovereignty needed to extend the authority of such institutions, both to command funds and to curb domestic rights violations with force, if necessary.

But even if this is the direction of global governance for the future, there remains a clear line, according to the political conception of justice, between the call for such institutions and a call for the institution of global socioeconomic justice. Everyone may have the right to live in a just society, but we do not have an obligation to live in a just society with everyone. The right to justice is the right that the society one lives in be justly governed. Any claims this creates against other societies and their members are distinctly secondary to those it creates against one's fellow citizens.

Is this stark division of levels of responsibility morally acceptable, or is it too radical an exclusion of humanity at large from full moral concern? The answer from the point of view of the political conception must be that there is no single level of full moral concern, because morality is essentially multilayered.

Even within the framework of a just society special obligations arise from contingent personal relations and voluntary associations or undertakings by individuals. The whole point of the political conception is that social justice itself is a rise in exclusive obligation, but with a broader associative range and from a lower moral baseline than the personal obligations. And it depends on the contingency of involuntary rather than voluntary association.

Perhaps this move to a new moral level can be best understood as a consequence of the more basic obligation, emphasized by both Hobbes and Kant, that all humans have to create and support a state of some kind—to leave and stay out of the state of nature. It is not an obligation to all other persons—in fact, it has no clear boundaries; it is merely an obligation to create the conditions of peace and a legal order, with whatever community offers itself.

This requirement is based not on a comprehensive value of equality, but on the imperative of securing basic rights, which can be done more or less locally. But once the state exists, we are in a new moral situation, where the value of equality has purchase. The difference between the political and the cosmopolitan conceptions is that the latter sees the formation of the state as answering also a universal demand for equality, even if as a practical matter it can be realized only locally. On the political conception, by contrast, the only universal requirement of equality is conditional in form: We are required to accord equal status to anyone with whom we are joined in a strong and coercively imposed political community.

Some standard of universalizability underlies even this conditional requirement. It is part of a multilayered conception of morality, shaped by the Kantian ideal of a kingdom of ends whose members do not share a common set of ends. The heightened obligations that arise from contingent particular associations do not subtract from a prior condition of universal concern, but rather move our moral relations selectively to a new level, at which more ends and responsibilities are shared. The universality of this morality consists in its applying to anyone who happens to be or to become a member of our society: No one is excluded in advance, and in that sense all persons are regarded as morally equal.

Such a morality also leaves space for voluntary combinations in the pursuit of common ends, which are not in general governed by standards of equality. But political institutions are different, because adherence to them is not voluntary: Emigration aside, one is not permitted to declare oneself not a member of one's society and not subject to its rules, and other members may coerce one's compliance if one tries to refuse. An institution that one has no choice about joining must offer terms of membership that meet a higher standard.

[VII]

My thoughts about this subject were kindled by Rawls's treatment of the ethics of international relations in *The Law of Peoples*, but his approach is different, so let me say something about it. First of all, he poses the question not as a general one about international obligations or global justice, but as a question about what principles should govern the foreign policy of a liberal society. So it is an elaboration of his account of a just society, rather than an independent account of a just world. And he sees the answer to this question as having to do primarily with how such a society should deal with the other societies with which it shares the world, whether these be liberal, or nonliberal but still "decent," in his term, or whether they be outlaw societies that fail to respect human rights and the restraints of international law.

As already noted, the moral units of this international morality are not individual human beings but separate societies, or "peoples," and it is equality among these collective units that is the basis of Rawls's conception. For that reason Charles Beitz has given it the name *social liberalism*, to contrast it with his own view, which he calls *cosmopolitan liberalism*.[15] Our obligations as members of a liberal society toward the members of other societies are not direct, but are filtered through the relations between our societies. That is because, as Rawls puts it, societies have a "moral nature" that deserves equal respect,

---

15. See the Afterword to the second edition of Charles Beitz, *Political Theory and International Relations* (Princeton, N.J.: Princeton University Press, 1999), 214–16; and "Rawls's Law of Peoples," Beitz's discussion in *Ethics* 110 (2000), 669–96.

provided they meet the basic conditions of decency. But individuals per se are not entitled to equal treatment internationally.

Rawls holds that the requirement of equal respect for other peoples is strong enough to impose on liberal societies a tolerance for nonliberal states that meet a minimal condition of decency, so that the foreign policy of a liberal state should not have the aim of moving all other societies toward liberalism, if possible. This is analogous to the restraint liberalism imposes internally against the use of state power to promote a particular comprehensive moral or religious view. It is surprising that internationally, equal respect should result precisely in toleration for the absence of such restraint in nonliberal societies. But Rawls believes that this consequence follows if we accord a moral nature and a moral right of equality to peoples that are not themselves derived from the moral equality of individuals, and that take precedence over domestic liberal values in the international case.

The claims of individuals take over only at a much lower threshold, that of basic human rights. A society that does not respect the human rights of its subjects forfeits, in Rawls's view, the moral status that demands respect, equality, and noninterference. But that is not necessarily true of a theocratic society with no elections, for example, provided it doesn't persecute minorities and observes due process of law.[16]

This seems to me a mistake. The political conception of justice need not be based on the strong personification of peoples and need not imply the principled toleration of nonliberal societies. I would take a more individualistic position than Rawls. The question of international toleration is difficult, but I believe that although there are obvious practical reasons for liberal societies not to try to impose liberal domestic justice universally, there are no moral reasons for restraint of the kind Rawls offers. It is more plausible to say that liberal states are not obliged either to tolerate nonliberal states or to try to transform them, because the duties of justice are essentially duties to our fellow citizens. But there seems nothing wrong with being particularly supportive of transformations in a liberal direction.

Whether other basic international obligations, such as those embodied in just war theory, can be accounted for without the moral personification of peoples is another question, but I would give a similar answer. People engaged in a legitimate collective enterprise deserve respect and noninterference, especially if it is an obligatory enterprise like the provision of security, law, and social peace. We owe it to other people—considered as individuals—to allow them, and to some degree enable them, to collectively help themselves. So respect

16. See his discussion of a decent hierarchical society in *The Law of Peoples*, 75–78.

for the autonomy of other societies can be thought of as respect for the human rights of their members, rather than as respect for the equality of peoples, taken as moral units in their own right.

Rawls's conception is that sovereignty is constrained internally by the moral equality of individuals who are subjects of the state, but that the same force does not operate externally: From outside, sovereignty is constrained by the moral equality of other peoples, which imposes requirements even on a state that does not owe their members what it owes its own. I am prepared to accept the first part of this claim, about the source of internal constraints, but would offer universal human rights rather than the equality of peoples or societies as the source of the constraints on the external exercise of sovereign power.[17]

[VIII]

The implications of the political conception for world politics tend to be conservative, but that is not the end of the story; the conservatism comes under pressure from powerful forces in the other direction. The source of that pressure lies both in existing global or international institutions and in the increasingly felt need to strengthen such institutions and to create new ones, for three types of purpose: the protection of human rights; the provision of humanitarian aid; and the provision of global public goods that benefit everyone, such as free trade, collective security, and environmental protection. Institutions that serve these purposes are not designed to extend democratic legitimacy and socioeconomic justice, but they naturally give rise to claims for both, in respect to their design and functioning. And they put pressure on national sovereignty by their need for power to be effective. They thus present a clearly perceived threat to the limits on claims of justice imposed by the political conception.

This poses a familiar dilemma: Prosperous nations have reasons to want more governance on a world scale, but they do not want the increased obligations and demands for legitimacy that may follow in its wake. They don't want to increase the range of those to whom they are obliged as they are toward their own citizens, and this reflects the convictions of their citizens, not just of their governments.

17. For a more broadly sympathetic discussion of Rawls's approach, see Stephen Macedo, "What Self-Governing Peoples Owe to One Another: Universalism, Diversity, and *The Law of Peoples*," *Fordham Law Review* 72 (2004), 1721–38. Macedo defends Rawls both on the refusal to extend distributive justice internationally and on the toleration of nonliberal peoples.

Resistance to the erosion of sovereignty has resulted in the U.S. refusal to join the Kyoto treaty on atmospheric emissions and the International Criminal Court, decisions that have been widely criticized. Similar questions arise over who is to determine the policies of the International Monetary Fund and the World Bank, and over the authority of the United Nations in matters of international peace and security. But by far the most important institutions from this point of view are those of the international economy itself.

The global economy, within which the familiar inequalities are now generated, requires a stable international system of property rights and contractual obligations that provide the conditions for international commerce. These include the rights of sovereign states to sell or confer legal title to the exploitation of their natural resources internationally; their right to borrow internationally and to create obligations of repayment on successor governments; the rights of commercial enterprises in one country to establish or acquire subsidiaries in other countries, and to profit from such investments; international extensions of antitrust law; regulation of financial markets to permit the orderly international flow of capital; the laws of patent and copyright; and the rules of international trade, including penalties for violations of agreed restrictions on protective tariffs, dumping, preferential subsidies, and so forth.[18] Many of the goods that contemporary persons consume, or their components, are produced in other countries. We are clearly in some kind of institutional relation—legal and economic—with people the world over.

This brings us to an issue that is internal to the political conception, rather than being about the choice between the political and the cosmopolitan conceptions. Some would argue that the present level of world economic interdependence already brings into force a version of the political conception of justice, so that Rawls's principles, or some alternative principles of distributive justice, are applicable over the domain covered by the existing cooperative institutions.[19] This would be a very strong result, but I believe that it is not the case, precisely because such institutions do not rise to the level of statehood.

The absence of sovereign authority over participant states and their members not only makes it practically infeasible for such institutions to pursue justice but makes them, under the political conception, an inappropriate site for claims of justice. For such claims to become applicable it is not enough that a number of individuals or groups be engaged in a collective activity that serves

---

18. Thomas Pogge places particular emphasis on the first two of these factors as sources of global responsibility, since they are so important in propping up authoritarian states that treat their own citizens unjustly.

19. See Brian Barry, *The Liberal Theory of Justice* (Oxford: Oxford University Press, 1973), 128–33; Beitz, *Political Theory and International Relations*, 150–53.

their mutual advantage. Mere economic interaction does not trigger the heightened standards of socioeconomic justice.

Current international rules and institutions may be the thin end of a wedge that will eventually expand to seriously dislodge the dominant sovereignty of separate nation-states, both morally and politically, but for the moment they lack something that according to the political conception is crucial for the application and implementation of standards of justice: They are not collectively enacted and coercively imposed in the name of all the individuals whose lives they affect, and they do not ask for the kind of authorization by individuals that carries with it a responsibility to treat all those individuals in some sense equally. Instead, they are set up by bargaining among mutually self-interested sovereign parties. International institutions act not in the name of individuals, but in the name of the states or state instruments and agencies that have created them. Hence the responsibility of those institutions toward individuals is filtered through the states that represent and bear primary responsibility for those individuals.

But while international governance falls far short of global sovereignty, and is ultimately dependent on the sovereignty of separate states, international institutions are not all alike. Some involve delegation of authority, by states, to a supranational institution, generally by treaty, where this amounts to a partial limitation of sovereignty. Under NAFTA, for example, the domestic courts of the United States, Canada, and Mexico are expected to enforce the judgments of its tribunals. And judgments of the European Court of Justice are enforced by the national courts of member states of the European Union.

Then there are the traditional international organizations, such as the UN, the WHO, the IMF, and the World Bank, which are controlled and financed by their member states and are empowered to act in various ways to pursue agreed-upon goals, but are not, with the exception of the Security Council, empowered to exercise coercive enforcement against states or individuals. Even the coercive authority of the Security Council is primarily a form of collective self-defense exercised by traditional sovereign powers, although there is some erosion of sovereignty in the move toward intervention to prevent domestic genocide.

Finally, there are a number of less formal structures that are responsible for a great deal of international governance—structures that have been enlighteningly described by Anne-Marie Slaughter in her recent book on government networks.[20] Such networks typically bring together officials of different countries with a common area of expertise and responsibility, who meet or

---

20. Anne-Marie Slaughter, *A New World Order* (Princeton, N.J.: Princeton University Press, 2004).

communicate regularly, harmonize their practices and policies, and operate by consensus, without having been granted decision-making authority by any treaty.

Examples are networks of environmental regulators, antitrust regulators, central bankers, finance ministers, securities commissioners, insurance supervisors, or police officials. The Basel Committee on Banking Supervision, for example, "is now composed of the representatives of thirteen central banks that regulate the world's largest banking markets."[21] It has developed standards for the division of tasks between home-country and host-country regulators, and has set uniform capital adequacy standards. Agreements are reached by consensus and implemented by the central banks themselves, acting under the sovereign authority of their several states. Slaughter argues that networks of this kind, which link the disaggregated subparts of sovereign states sharing common competences and responsibilities rather than the (notionally) unitary states themselves, will become increasingly important in global governance, and should be recognized as the wave of the future.

It is a convincing case. It is important to recognize that the traditional model of international organizations based on treaties between sovereign states has been transcended. Nevertheless, I believe that the newer forms of international governance share with the old a markedly indirect relation to individual citizens and that this is morally significant. All these networks bring together representatives not of individuals, but of state functions and institutions. Those institutions are responsible to their own citizens and may have a significant role to play in the support of social justice for those citizens. But a global or regional network does not have a similar responsibility of social justice for the combined citizenry of all the states involved, a responsibility that if it existed would have to be exercised collectively by the representatives of the member states. Rather, the aim of such institutions is to find ways in which the member states, or state-parts, can cooperate to better advance their separate aims, which will presumably include the pursuit of domestic social justice in some form. Very importantly, they rely for enforcement on the power of the separate sovereign states, not of a supranational force responsible to all.

Individuals are not the constituents of such institutions. Even if the more powerful states are motivated to some extent by humanitarian concerns to shape the rules in consideration of the weakest and poorest members of the international community, that does not change the situation fundamentally. Justice is not merely the pursuit of common aims by unequal parties whose self-interest is softened by charity. Justice, on the political conception, requires

---

21. Slaughter, *A New World Order*, 43.

a collectively imposed social framework, enacted in the name of all those governed by it, and aspiring to command their acceptance of its authority even when they disagree with the substance of its decisions.

Justice applies, in other words, only to a form of organization that claims political legitimacy and the right to impose decisions by force, and not to a voluntary association or contract among independent parties concerned to advance their common interests. I believe this holds even if the natural incentives to join such an association, and the costs of exit, are substantial, as is true of some international organizations and agreements. There is a difference between voluntary association, however strongly motivated, and coercively imposed collective authority.

[IX]

A second, somewhat different objection to this limitation of justice to the nation-state is that it assumes an unrealistically sharp dichotomy between sovereign states and existing global institutions with respect to agency, authorization, and authority. So even if economic globalization doesn't trigger the full standards of social justice, it entails them in a modified form.

In fact, according to this objection, there is a sliding scale of degrees of comembership in a nested or sometimes overlapping set of governing institutions, of which the state is only the most salient. If we accept the moral framework of the political conception, we should conclude that there is a corresponding spectrum of degrees of egalitarian justice, which we owe to our fellow participants in these collective structures in proportion to our degrees of joint responsibility for and subjection to their authority. My relation of comembership in the system of international trade with the Brazilian who grows my coffee or the Philippine worker who assembles my computer is weaker than my relation of comembership in U.S. society with the Californian who picks my lettuce or the New Yorker who irons my shirts. But doesn't the first pair of relations as well as the second justify concern about the moral arbitrariness of the inequalities that arise through our joint participation in this system? One may even see an appeal to such a value in the call for standards of minimum compensation, fair labor practices, and protection of worker health and safety as conditions on international trade agreements—even if the real motivation behind it is protectionism against cheap third world labor.

Perhaps such a theory of justice as a "continuous" function of degrees of collective responsibility could be worked out. It is in fact a natural suggestion, in light of the general theory that morality is multilayered. But I doubt that the rules of international trade rise to the level of collective action needed to trigger demands for justice, even in diluted form. The relation remains essentially one of bargaining, until a leap has been made to the creation of collectively authorized sovereign authority.[22]

On the "discontinuous" political conception I am defending, international treaties or conventions, such as those that set up the rules of trade, have a quite different moral character from contracts between self-interested parties within a sovereign state. The latter may be part of a just socioeconomic system because of the background of collectively imposed property and tax law in which they are embedded. But contracts between sovereign states have no such background: They are "pure" contracts, and nothing guarantees the justice of their results. They are like the contracts favored by libertarians, but unless one accepts the libertarian conception of legitimacy, the obligations they create are not and need not be underwritten by any kind of socioeconomic justice. They are more primitive than that.

On the political conception, the same is true of the economic relation in which I stand to Brazilian or Philippine workers. Within our respective societies the contracts and laws on which this relation depends are subject to standards of social justice. Insofar as they transcend societal boundaries, however, the requirements of background justice are filtered out and commercial relations become instead something much thinner: instruments for the common pursuit of self-interest. The representatives of distinct societies that establish the framework within which such transactions can be undertaken will be guided by the interests of their own members, including their interest in domestic social justice. But a more comprehensive criterion of global socioeconomic justice is not part of the picture. Globalization may threaten domestic justice in the rich countries, but it does so through market forces, not through global justice.

By contrast a "continuous" or sliding scale of requirements of justice would have to depend on a scale of degrees of collective engagement. I am related to the person who assembled my computer in the Philippines through the combination of U.S. and Philippine property, commercial, and labor law; the international currency markets; the international application of patent law; and the agreements on trade overseen by the World Trade Organization. The claim would have to be that since we are both participating members of this network of institutions, this puts us in the same boat for purposes of raising issues of justice, but somehow a different and perhaps leakier boat than that created by a common nation-state.

---

22. This now seems to me the most doubtful claim in the paper. For a persuasive response, see Joshua Cohen and Charles Sabel, "Extra Rempublicam, Nulla Justitia?" *Philosophy and Public Affairs* 34 (2006), 147–75.

Leaving aside the practical problems of implementing even a weaker standard of economic justice through such institutions, does the idea make moral sense? Is there a plausible position covering this case that is intermediate between the political and the cosmopolitan conceptions? (The cosmopolitan conception would say that ideally, the full standards of justice should apply, but that practically, they cannot be implemented given the limited power of international institutions.) Although it is far from clear what the answer is, it seems to me that such a sliding standard of obligation is considerably less plausible than either the cosmopolitan (one-place) or political (two-place) standard. It is supposed to be a variation on the political conception, according to which one can be moved above the default position defined by human rights and collective self-interest through participation in the institutional structures that make complex economic interaction possible. But if those institutions do not act in the name of all the individuals concerned, and are sustained by those individuals only through the agency of their respective governments or branches of those governments, what is the characteristic in virtue of which they create obligations of justice and presumptions in favor of equal consideration for all those individuals? If the default really is a basic humanitarianism, permitting voluntary interaction for the pursuit of common interests, then something more is needed to move us up toward the higher standard of equal consideration. It will not emerge merely from cooperation and the conventions that make cooperation possible.

I would add two qualifications to this rather uncompromising claim. First, there are good reasons, not deriving from global socioeconomic justice, to be concerned about the consequences of economic relations with states that are *internally* egregiously unjust. Even if internal justice is the primary responsibility of each state, the complicity of other states in the active support or perpetuation of an unjust regime is a secondary offense against justice.

Second, even self-interested bargaining between states should be tempered by considerations of humanity, and the best way of doing this in the present world is to allow poor societies to benefit from their comparative advantage in labor costs to become competitors in world markets. WTO negotiations have finally begun to show some sense that it is indecent, for example, when subsidies by wealthy nations to their own farmers cripple the market for agricultural products from developing countries, both for export and domestically.

[X]

That is more or less where we are now. But I said there was a dilemma, stemming from the need for more effective global institutions to deal with our collective problems, from global warming to free trade. It is not only the fear of tyranny but also the resistance to expanded democracy, expanded demands for legitimacy, and expanded scope for the claims of justice that inhibits the development of powerful supranational institutions. Fortunate nations, at any rate, fear such developments. They therefore face the problem of how to create a global order that will have its own legitimacy, but not the kind of legitimacy that undermines the strict limits on their responsibilities.[23]

The resistance to expanded democracy is sometimes explained on the ground that the right kind of *demos* does not exist internationally to permit democratic government beyond the nation-state. Even in the subglobal and much less unequal space of Europe this is a serious problem, which has given rise to significant debate. If there is not now a European civil society, is there nevertheless the hope of one? Is the possibility compatible with the linguistic diversity of Europe? Could it perhaps be brought into existence as the *result* of democratic European political institutions, rather than serving as a precondition of their creation?

But this, I believe, is not the main issue. Multilingual and multinational states have their problems, and they may have functioned most successfully before the era of democracy. But if there came into being a genuine European federation with some form of democratically elected representative government, politics would eventually develop on a European scale to compete for control of this centralized power. The real problem is that any such government would be subject to claims of legitimacy and justice that are more than the several European populations are willing to submit themselves to. That reflects in part a conviction that they are not morally obliged to expand their moral vulnerabilities in this way. (The recent expansion of the European Union, by increasing its economic inequality, will almost certainly inhibit the growth of its federal power for just this reason.)

Globally, there are a number of ways in which greater international authority would be desirable. Resources for development aid and emergency relief could be more effectively obtained by a systematic assessment or tax than by the present system of voluntary contributions. Global public goods like atmospheric protection and free trade could obviously benefit from increased international authority. Both the protection of human rights and the provision of basic humanitarian aid would be easier if regimes found to be responsible for the oppression or destitution of their own subjects in these respects were regarded as having forfeited their sovereign rights against outside interference.

23. The undemocratic rulers of many poor nations have strong reasons of a different kind to protect their sovereign authority against international encroachment, but that is another topic.

Not only the prevention of genocide but the relief of famine may sometimes require a change of government, and the intervention of collective outside forces and agencies. This would mean establishing a link between internal and external legitimacy, as a qualification of the general right of noninterference.[24]

But all these types of increased international authority would bring with them increased responsibilities. An authority capable of carrying out these functions and imposing its decisions would naturally be subject to claims of legitimacy, pressures toward democracy, and pressures to apply standards of justice in the distribution of burdens and benefits through its policies. There is a big difference between agreements or consensus among separate states committed to the advancement of their own interests and a binding procedure, based on some kind of collective authority, charged with securing the common good. The potential costs are much more serious than the risks that led to the U.S. refusal to join the International Criminal Court.

This leaves us with the question whether some form of legitimacy is possible for the global or international case that does not depend on supranational sovereignty or democracy—let alone distributive justice—and yet can be embodied in institutions that are less cumbersome and feeble than those that depend for their creation and functioning on unanimous voluntary acceptance by sovereign states. For the moment, I do not see such a possibility, though perhaps it can be invented. The alternative to global sovereignty may not be global anarchy, but a clear and limited form of such governance remains elusive.

[XI]

Yet in thinking about the future, we should keep in mind that political power is rarely created as a result of demands for legitimacy, and that there is little reason to think that things will be different in this case.

If we look at the historical development of conceptions of justice and legitimacy for the nation-state, it appears that sovereignty usually precedes legitimacy. First, there is the concentration of power; then, gradually, there grows a demand for consideration of the interests of the governed, and for giving them a greater voice in the exercise of power. The demand may be reformist, or it may be revolutionary, or it may be a demand for reform made credible by the threat of revolution, but it is the existence of concentrated sovereign power that

---

24. For a forceful statement of this view, see Brian Barry, "Statism and Nationalism: A Cosmopolitan Critique," in *Global Justice*, Nomos 41, ed. Ian Shapiro and Lea Brilmayer (New York: New York University Press, 1999), 12–65.

prompts the demand, and makes legitimacy an issue. War may result in the destruction of a sovereign power, leading to reconfigurations of sovereignty in response to claims of legitimacy, but even in that case the conquerors who exercise power become the targets of those claims.

Even in the most famous case of the creation of a democratic federation, illegitimacy preceded legitimacy. The foundation of the United States depended on the protection of slavery, without which unanimity among the thirteen ex-colonies could not have been achieved. In fighting the Civil War to preserve the Union, Lincoln knew that the preservation of sovereign power over the entire territory was the essential condition for progress in the pursuit of democratic legitimacy and justice. The battle for more political and social equality has continued ever since, but it has been possible only because centralized power was kept in existence, so that people could contest the legitimacy of the way it was being used.

So I close with a speculation. While it is conceivable in theory that political authority should be created in response to an antecedent demand for legitimacy, I believe this is unlikely to happen in practice. What is more likely is the increase and deployment of power in the interests of those who hold it, followed by a gradual growth of pressure to make its exercise more just, and to free its organization from the historical legacy of the balance of forces that went into its creation. Unjust and illegitimate regimes are the necessary precursors of the progress toward legitimacy and democracy, because they create the centralized power that can then be contested, and perhaps turned in other directions without being destroyed. For this reason, I believe the most likely path toward some version of global justice is through the creation of patently unjust and illegitimate global structures of power that are tolerable to the interests of the most powerful current nation-states. Only in that way will institutions come into being that are worth taking over in the service of more democratic purposes, and only in that way will there be something concrete for the demand for legitimacy to go to work on.

This point is independent of the dispute between the political and cosmopolitan conceptions. We are unlikely to see the spread of global justice in the long run unless we first create strong supranational institutions that do not aim at justice but that pursue common interests and reflect the inequalities of bargaining power among existing states. The question is whether these conditions can be realized by units established through voluntary agreement rather than by involuntary imposition. The path of conquest, responsible for so much of the scope of sovereign authority in the past, is no longer an option on a large scale. Other historical developments would have to create the illegitimate concentrations of power that can nurture demands for legitimacy, and provide them with something that is both worth taking over and not too easy to break up.

My conclusion, though it presupposes a conception of justice that Hobbes did not accept, is Hobbesian in spirit: The path from anarchy to justice must go through injustice. It is often unclear whether, for a given problem, international anarchy is preferable to international injustice. But if we accept the political conception, the global scope of justice will expand only through developments that first increase the injustice of the world by introducing effective but illegitimate institutions to which the standards of justice apply, standards by which we may hope they will eventually be transformed. An example, perhaps, of the cunning of history.

7

The Limits of
International Law

Jeremy Rabkin's book, *Law without Nations?*[1] is a forceful defense of
the virtues of national sovereignty and of the claim that American constitutional government places strict limits on the reach and authority
of international law. In part, Rabkin is responding to critics of the
unilateralism of the Bush administration—its rejection of the Kyoto
Treaty, its refusal to join the International Criminal Court, its invasion of Iraq without explicit Security Council authorization—but the
interest of the book is much broader than that. It takes up one of the
most important questions we face about the direction of the world,
and it compares the merits of the internationalist answer to that question embodied in the ideals of the European Union, and the more
nationalist answer represented by the conduct of the United States
and (according to Rabkin) by its entire historical and constitutional
tradition.

The sovereign nation-state has existed for only a few centuries,
and some people think it is on its way out, but it has proved an exceptionally effective and conceptually transparent human creation. As the
Dutch legal theorist Grotius explained in the seventeenth century, a
sovereign power is one that has legal authority over a domain but is
not subject to any higher human authority. And legal authority means,
in this context, the authority to make law and to enforce it, by virtue of

---

1. Jeremy Rabkin, *Law without Nations? Why Constitutional Government Requires Sovereign
States* (Princeton, N.J.: Princeton University Press, 2005).

an actual monopoly of coercive power together with the general acceptance, by those governed, of the sovereign's exclusive right to employ it.

This consent of the governed may be given for many reasons, ranging from reverence or fear to the desire for security, freedom, and the pursuit of happiness, and it may be given to sovereigns of many forms, from monarchies and theocracies to democratic republics. In our case it attaches itself to a specific form of constitutional government. The liberal justification for sovereign power is still, in our own day, a form of social contract. We accept the authority and the coercive power of a procedurally constrained and substantively limited system of collective control because it is the best way for a large population to live together in peace, to prosper, and to further common interests and values, while retaining substantial freedom as individuals to pursue the many values that they do not share.

Constitutional sovereignty requires a national population whose interests and values are sufficiently compatible to permit common allegiance to a single legal authority for the settlement of their inevitable conflicts over what the rules should be to which everyone is subjected. This is a precious resource, difficult to achieve. It depends, as we know, on historical contingencies of various kinds. Rabkin believes that for the nations that are fortunate enough to have it, constitutional sovereign authority puts a natural upper bound on the sources of law. We cannot find its equivalent, he argues, at the international level, where there is not—and cannot be—a comparable social contract.

This does not mean there can be no international law, but international law has to be very different from the law of a sovereign state. It must be agreed on and enforced by the separate sovereign powers themselves, and it will therefore be much more limited in its capacity to settle conflicts among them. Where a common rule will serve all their interests, as with rules governing trade, or the treatment of prisoners of war, independent sovereign states can enter into agreements that are enforceable by retaliation. The reason to abide by them is that if one state defects, others can do the same, and everyone, including the initial defector, will lose. By contrast, says Rabkin,

> A sovereign state imposes law in a quite different way. It does not need anything like unanimous or general agreement—among its own citizens—before it proclaims its own law. And for most purposes, the state is the enforcer, not the citizens.... A sovereign has the right to make and enforce law and the citizens are obliged to obey, even if they dislike the law and even if they do not approve the way the law is implemented or enforced against others.

And Rabkin adds, "If international law could be enforced on dissenters, in the manner of domestic law, then the dissenting states would no longer be sovereign. Not many states (or their peoples) would consent to yield up their independence in this way to outside powers."

This makes it clear why there is no prospect of a world state. But that leaves us with a further question: How much international law is it desirable and possible for a world of separate sovereign states to create, without creating a world state? For the reasons Rabkin gives, it would have to be law whose enforcement was left in the hands of existing nation-states, even though its content was determined by some procedure whose authority they were all prepared to accept—presumably with the authorization of their citizens.

This is where opinions diverge. Rabkin believes that even in areas of undeniably common interest, such as protecting the environment or preserving peace, international conflicts of interest and of fundamental values are generally too great to permit the creation of such a procedure. Treaties, rather than anything resembling legislation, must remain the primary sources of international law. But why can't a treaty itself delegate authority to an international decision-making body, voluntarily diminishing the sovereign authority of its national parties without creating a supersovereign?

This is what seems to have happened with the formation of the European Union. The EU is neither a true federation, with final sovereign power over the member states, nor a traditional treaty, with the members retaining their full sovereignty. The states have delegated some of their legal authority to its administrative and legal institutions, but enforcement rests in their own hands, and any state is free to withdraw from the Union.

Rabkin gives the EU a good deal of attention, because he thinks that it is a very bad model for world governance on a broader scale, and that it expresses the failure of European political opinion to appreciate the liberal conditions of legitimacy, which require that legal authority not float free of political accountability.

> Perhaps the European Union has found a stable and constitutionally acceptable formula for imposing supranational law. There is, in fact, much reason to doubt that it will prove stable and it certainly does not conform to American ideas of constitutional government. But in any case, the European Union remains a very special sort of international institution. The international community at large has very little capacity to impose its will on individual states with the same reliability as the bureaucrats of Brussels.

If the EU succeeds, it will be because the attachment of Europeans to common interests and values is strong enough to contain the conflicts of interest that will inevitably remain—and without the benefit of a centralized monopoly of force. If it fails, and remains essentially a free-trade zone, it will be because of popular unwillingness to share sovereignty with two dozen other nations— a sentiment manifest in the 2005 French and Dutch rejections of the EU Constitution.

On a global scale, the consensus required to sustain a legal system of this type is out of the question. There is only one area where the recognized strength of common interest has come reliably to outweigh the divisive effects of conflicts of interest: the promotion of free trade. Since economic interests are so powerful, the World Trade Organization has the potential to sustain a form of global governance that will limit the sovereignty of states. As Rabkin observes, "Unlike other international institutions, the WTO can condemn an American statute and get the United States government to change it." The reason is that, although its provisions are treaties entered into by unanimous agreement of the parties, their interpretation and application are not left to the discretion of the parties but are assigned to the organization itself.

The Appellate Body that has final authority in the disposition of complaints arising from WTO agreements has declared that its interpretations will make reference to "general principles of international law." This opens the way to using trade litigation as a lever to implement social, environmental, and human rights goals. As Rabkin remarks, "Once it is accepted that trade may be conditioned on compliance with domestic environmental or social norms, there is no obvious limit to what can be imposed," and he invokes the example of the Interstate Commerce Clause of the Constitution as a basis for Supreme Court approval of almost anything Congress decides to regulate. (The WTO may not go that far, but anyone who doubts the power of economic leverage should contemplate the remarkable spectacle of Turkey's abolishing the death penalty and passing laws against sexual harassment and marital rape, in order to become a candidate for membership in the EU.)

Rabkin's principle of legitimacy is strongly opposed to piggybacking a world legal order on economic globalization:

> One may think the world needs a great deal of international regulation. It does not follow that the world is now organized to provide a constitutional framework for agreeing on the proper content and direction for such regulation.... A world which has moved beyond sovereignty is a world which has moved beyond the premises of liberalism and beyond the premises of constitutional government, in any traditional understanding of that term.

He would prefer that the most divisive international issues not be governed by law at all than that they be subject to a form of international law that lacks a sound foundation.

For this reason, Rabkin is opposed both to the International Criminal Court and to the presumption that military intervention requires UN authorization. The ICC preempts the right of a state to enact an amnesty, as so many have done, in the course of a transition from dictatorship to democracy. And the United Nations has been extremely reluctant to authorize military action to stop even the most horrible massacres. Decisions on such issues, he believes, are better left in the hands of sovereign states, acting individually or jointly. There will be bad decisions, but fewer, and some of them will be made by democratically accountable governments.

Those who want to argue for the legitimacy of much more international regulation than Rabkin favors must do two things. First, they must identify the sources of international law that can take us beyond self-enforcing treaties or conventions unanimously adopted by sovereign states. Second, they must describe the institutions and procedures by which these rules are to be identified, applied, and enforced—even against states that do not accept them.

If we look at the range of moral and political values that command allegiance in the world today, this seems an impossibly tall order. There are, of course, international conventions on human rights, but as Rabkin rightly observes, they do not mean much when China is a signatory to the Covenant on Civil and Political Rights and Saudi Arabia is a signatory to the Convention against Torture, with the reservation that it does not cover bodily mutilation as a form of punishment, as demanded by *sharia*. Even if there is a developing convergence of enlightened opinion on certain norms, Rabkin is right to insist that such norms are not law.

The internationalist has to argue that legitimate and effective world standards will come into being only if we commit ourselves collectively to institutions with the authority to implement them. Only in this way will we give ourselves the incentive to hammer them out together and take them seriously. We have to take some risks, and accept the possibility of finding ourselves on the losing side of some arguments, in order to move ahead with the urgently needed increase in global regulation.

The International Criminal Court seems to me the best candidate for the role of a hopeful mutation of this sort. It will presumably be firmly in the hands of jurists committed to human rights and the rule of law, whose interpretive disagreements will stay within a range broadly acceptable to the Western democracies. It does not seem very risky to give such an institution the chance to develop an international form of common-law jurisprudence, based on existing conventions sharpened by moral and legal interpretation.

But many people believe that the United States should also show much more deference to the United Nations, because that is the only way the UN can hope to develop the authority it needs to make the world safer for everyone. On this view, invading Iraq without a second Security Council resolution would have been very wrong even if there had in fact been all those weapons of mass destruction and the United States had provided enough troops to pacify the country after the removal of Saddam Hussein.

There is a chicken-and-egg problem here. Authority exists only if it is accepted, but it will be accepted only if it is seen as legitimate, in virtue of the way it is exercised. It requires a leap of faith to accept the authority of the UN and then hope that it will earn this acceptance by its decisions. In matters of war, peace, and humanitarian intervention, the leap may be too large to be reasonable. Unlike Rabkin, I regret the unavailability of a sound basis for the significant transcendence of sovereignty by international law, but I must agree with him that in the most important cases that is the situation.

Law without Nations is readable and persuasive. It includes an instructive history of theories of sovereignty and international law from the sixteenth century onward, and much interesting material on the role of such ideas in the formation and subsequent history of the United States. I was put off by the relentless tone of contempt for those who hold other views. Rabkin cannot forgive Europe for the Holocaust—why should he? But he brings it into the discussion repeatedly in ways that strain the sense of relevance. He sees in the present European appeal for peaceful conflict resolution a parallel with the acquiescence of German satellites in Western Europe after 1940 to the New Order imposed by the Third Reich—no coincidence that Israel now, like the Jews then, is an object of hatred seen as an obstacle to harmony. He says Europeans who want Israel to dismantle its settlements in the West Bank should shrink from endorsing the notion that those territories must be *Judenrein*. And of the failure of Dutch UN peacekeepers to prevent the massacre at Srebrenica in 1995 he says, "It should not have been very surprising. In 1940, the Dutch relied on international law for their protection and were overrun by Germany in a matter of hours. A Dutch resistance movement did not develop for several years—well after the Dutch allowed their Jewish fellow citizens to be rounded up for extermination." But the Serbs offered fierce partisan resistance to the Nazis. Does that have any bearing on what we should think about Serbs murdering their Muslim fellow citizens half a century later?

Rabkin demonstrates that in our world constitutional sovereignty provides the indispensable basis for both domestic and international law. Yet it is essential that this not be interpreted to license every untrammeled exercise of sovereign power and a disregard for the vital role of reciprocity in international affairs. Sovereign authority does not excuse the unilateralism of the Bush administration in trying to evade the requirements of the incontestably valid Geneva Convention on treatment of prisoners of war, not to mention prohibitions against torture. Such rules do not impair the nation's sovereignty, and flouting them has done it great damage. If only sovereign nations can create a decent world, then decency must begin at home.

8

Appiah's Rooted Cosmopolitanism

In two recent books Kwame Anthony Appiah undertakes to combine a form of liberalism that aspires to universal validity with a full recognition and substantial acceptance of the important cultural and ethical diversity that characterizes our world. *The Ethics of Identity*[1] is a philosopher's contribution to ethical theory, *Cosmopolitanism*[2] is a more popular work of social and political reflection, but both are of wide interest—invitingly written and enlivened by personal history.

Some of the issues Appiah addresses are familiar from contemporary public debate over multiculturalism, the relation of the state to religious pluralism, the effects of economic globalization, and the international reach of universal standards of human rights. Most of us have our own reactions to the prohibition of the Islamic headscarf in French *lycées* and Turkish universities, restrictions on English signage in Quebec, the battles over gay marriage, the teaching of evolution in American public schools, the practice of female circumcision in Africa, the return of the Elgin Marbles to Greece, or the claim that liberal rights should be regarded merely as an ethnic custom of the West. Appiah is wonderfully perceptive and level-headed about this tangle of issues.

1. Kwame Anthony Appiah, *The Ethics of Identity* (Princeton, N.J.: Princeton University Press, 2005).

2. Kwame Anthony Appiah, *Cosmopolitanism* (New York: W. W. Norton, 2006).

His central claim is developed from the pluralistic liberalism of John Stuart Mill. Even though individual lives are what really matter, those lives and their value depend on identities of many different kinds shaped by the thick web of diverse cultures, religions, associations, and practices that make real, existing human beings. A theory of human good cannot be based on an abstract universal concept of the human—either biological or metaphysical—because humanity alone is not a sufficient identity for any of us. We are all much more concrete and specific and embedded than that.

Appiah has more identities than most of us. Born to a Ghanaian father and an English mother, nephew of the king of Asante and grandson of a British chancellor of the exchequer, brought up in Africa and educated in England, he now teaches at Princeton and is a leading figure in the academic establishments of philosophy and African-American studies. His parents were Methodists but some of his relatives are Muslim and many of them believe in witchcraft. And he is gay. Appiah may insist that such complexity is not rare, but it has given him a greater sense of freedom than I suspect is felt by people whose identities are simpler. This puts him in a particularly strong position to explain why individualistic liberalism is not inevitably at war with parochial identities, even though some identities can be oppressive or even crippling. Appiah is as cosmopolitan as it is possible to be, but he has maintained his local roots in full consciousness and espouses a form of liberal multiculturalism that he calls "rooted cosmopolitanism."

The view is developed at three levels: the individual, the societal, and the global or universal. Like Mill, Appiah believes that the individual level provides the foundation. Some of what is good and bad for human beings is determined by our animal biology alone, but the essentially human goods depend on identities that are determined by each individual's membership in smaller groups or systems of human relations. Think how important a person's family, profession, native language, or religion is in determining what it is for his life to go well.

These sources of value can also be a source of trouble, of course. Appiah applies a distinction made by Ronald Dworkin between circumstances that are *parameters* for determining what would constitute a successful life, and circumstances that are *limits*—"obstacles that get in the way of our making the ideal life that the parameters help define." It illuminates the problematic ethics of identity when we notice that some of the most politically salient identities function both as parameters and as limits, and that there are struggles at both the individual and the societal level over how to categorize them.

At one time, the dominant liberal response to social contempt or demeaning stereotypes attached to blacks, gays, or women was to deny the ethical significance of such identities altogether—an attitude expressed in the embarrassing modifier "...who happens to be black." But this has been displaced in our time by the effort to turn them from limits into parameters:

> An African American after the Black Power movement takes the old script of self-hatred, the script in which he or she is a nigger, and works, in community with others, to construct a series of positive black life-scripts. In these life-scripts, being a Negro is recoded as being black: and this requires, among other things, refusing to assimilate to white norms of speech and behavior.... It will not even be enough to be treated with equal dignity despite being black: for that would suggest that being black counts to some degree against one's dignity. And so one will end up asking to be respected *as a black.*

Appiah tells the same story about gay identity after Stonewall. But he then adds:

> Demanding respect for people *as blacks* and *as gays* can go along with notably rigid strictures as to how one is to be an African American or a person with same-sex desires.... It is at this point that someone who takes autonomy seriously may worry whether we have replaced one kind of tyranny with another.

A further problem with black solidarity in particular is that it relies on a dubious criterion of identity. Many Americans believe that a person with one African American and one European parent is an African American. If this principle is reapplied consistently, it results in the "one-drop rule," according to which *any* African ancestry makes one black. But Appiah cites statistical studies showing that millions of Americans who look white and are regarded by themselves and others as white have ancestors who were African slaves— that these may even outnumber those who regard themselves as black. If that is so, then the ordinary conception of black identity is incoherent.

This argument may impose too much logic on a vague concept, but it makes an important point. In trying to turn the tables on racism, the civil rights movement and black solidarity have not challenged the conceptual racism associated with the one-drop rule and may thereby be missing an opportunity to undermine the grip of the categories themselves:

> Current U.S. practices presuppose, by and large, that there is a fact of the matter about everyone as to whether or not she is African American. One is required to fill in forms for all sorts of purposes

that fix one's race, and other people—arresting police officers, for example—may be required to do so as well.... Were the government to modify these practices, it would remove at least one tiny strut that gives support to the idea that social conceptions of race are consistent with reality.

Appiah's position is not that individual autonomy requires freeing ourselves of thick identities, but that we have to consider their constraining as well as their enabling effects, and even their rationality, in deciding how to be who we are.

Appiah poses the societal question this way: "What claims, if any, can identity groups as such justly make upon the state?" His answer, basically, is "none." Groups have no inherent moral standing; their importance depends on their importance to the lives of individuals. Appiah resists Charles Taylor's claim that the value of a culture is not derivative from its value to individuals, but the reverse.

Whatever may be the political implications, I think that he is here taking ethical individualism too far, and that Taylor is on to something important. When a language and its literature, or a musical or artistic form, or even a cuisine or a game, dies out, so that no one is able any longer to appreciate or to practice it, something valuable has gone out of existence. This cannot be explained by the harm to existing individuals, all of whom will have other things to do and other ways to flourish. Even though the lost element of culture could have continued only in the lives of individuals, its absence is not a loss to them if they do not miss it. It is the recognition that its disappearance would be a loss nonetheless, though a loss to no one, that motivates some of the strongest desires for cultural preservation, however quixotic. (I sympathize completely with the lament of a classicist I know that students at Oxford are no longer required to write Greek and Latin verse.)

Appiah shares with Mill an insistence on the value of social diversity to permit the flourishing of different individuals, and a distaste for uniformity. But like Mill, he thinks this means that some forms of diversity should not be tolerated: "It may be that many of us value diversity not because it is a primordial good but because we take it to be a correlative of liberty, of nondomination. But if autonomy is the sponsoring concern, the diversity principle—the value of diversity *simpliciter*—cannot command our loyalty." So he is not sympathetic to the kind of anthropological relativism that supports the protection of traditional group practices even if they impose serious disadvantages or inequalities on some members of the group (often its female members, as with arranged early marriage). And he denies that the mere legal possibility of exit from such a group is sufficient to immunize it from societal oversight to protect the individual rights of its members. The right of exit is not enough to cancel the constraining power of strong communal identities. What the state should do, however, depends on how fundamental the competing claims are: Appiah would not require the Catholic Church to admit women to the priesthood.

Appiah is also unsympathetic to preservationism, the obligation of a society to help identity groups, cultural or linguistic, ensure their survival into succeeding generations—which goes beyond its obligation to see that present members of those groups do not suffer discrimination or persecution. Individual autonomy trumps group preservation, just as it does in the case of arranged marriages:

> The ethical principles of equal dignity that underlie liberal thinking
> seem to militate against allowing the parents their way because
> we care about the autonomy of these young women. If this is true
> in the individual case, it seems to me equally true where a whole
> generation of one group wishes to impose a form of life on the next
> generation—and a fortiori true if they seek to impose it somehow on
> still later generations.
>
> And once we attend to these vistas of descent, it may strike us
> that culture talk is not so very far from the race talk that it would
> supplant in liberal discourse.

He concludes that for linguistic minorities, like the Québecois, it is political inclusion rather than community preservation that the state should aim at, and let the chips fall where they may.

Appiah is very good on the confusing issue of the "neutrality" of the state in a pluralistic liberal society. Since this is an evaluative concept, it cannot mean general value neutrality, but must mean neutrality among a certain subset of values and practices based on a nonneutral evaluative premise. Appiah believes that a requirement of equal respect for individuals underlies such neutrality as liberalism requires—among religions, conceptions of the good life, sexual mores, and so forth. But respect for individuals and their autonomy will rule out respect for identities that undermine it, and the liberal state, while it will not engage in the formation of souls to a single standard, will try to impose through education and public forms of equality the conditions for pluralistic self-realization.

Equal respect is required of the state, but not of individuals, whose personal associations and communal identities essentially involve exclusive attachments without which life would be impoverished and abstract: "A radical egalitarian might give his money to the poor, but he can't give his friends to the friendless." Or, "to put the matter paradoxically: impartiality is a strictly position-dependent obligation. What is a virtue in a referee is not a virtue in a prize-fighter's wife."

The final level of Appiah's analysis is the world as a whole. He is not a moral relativist; he believes in universal human rights. There is objective truth, not only in science but in morality—though this doesn't guarantee that we will all come to agree on it. But he does not think this points to a utopian crusade to bring the world under the authority of a single standard—as other visions of objective universal truth—Christian, Muslim, Marxist—have too often hoped. He believes that the pluralistic liberalism that permits coexistence within liberal states can find its counterpart for the world. This is partly because what is universal hardly exhausts the truth:

> Identity is at the heart of human life: liberalism...takes this picture
> seriously, and tries to construct a state and society that take account
> of the ethics of identity without losing sight of the values of personal
> autonomy. But the cosmopolitan impulse is central to this view, too,
> because it sees a world of cultural and social variety as a precondition
> for the self-creation that is at the heart of a meaningful human life.

What is universal, though immensely important, merely provides a protective framework for the flourishing of individuality. And we can come to agree on certain basic protections in practice without starting from a common theoretical foundation. (Here Appiah invokes Cass Sunstein's constitutional theory of "incompletely theorized agreements.") The key to coexistence and mutual benefit from the variety of forms of life is familiarity, and not just reason. We have to get used to one another, and then over time our habits will evolve. Sheer exposure can accomplish a great deal. That, he points out, is how attitudes toward homosexuality have been transformed in our own society. And it may eventually have its effect on the "woman question" that he thinks plays a large part in fueling Islamic hostility to the West.

It is a humane and optimistic vision, eloquently expressed. Disarmingly, Appiah describes his view at one point as "wishy-washy cosmopolitanism," and if these books have a fault, it is that of underrating the depth of the conflicts that make the spread of liberalism so difficult. Appiah's golden rule of cosmopolitanism is a famous quotation from the comic playwright Terence, a former North African slave who lived and wrote in Rome: "I am human: nothing human is alien to me." Though he acknowledges that pessimists "can cite a dismal litany to the contrary," Appiah believes that the accumulation of changes in individual consciousness brought on by communication and mobility is already propelling us along this upward path. He rejects by implication the "clash of civilizations" as the global drama to which we are all condemned. I hope the future will prove him right, though the experience of our time makes me wonder. Reflecting on the fact that it took centuries of bloodshed for the West to move from the wars of religion to its present roughly liberal consensus, I do not expect to live long enough to find out.

9

Sandel and the Paradox
of Liberalism

[I]

The political system of the United States manages to contain, under conditions of peace if not civility, a remarkable range of moral, ideological, and religious conflicts. The conflicts are not so severe as those that led to the Civil War, but they are greater than those that divide most European countries—where public opinion occupies a narrower political range, and religion is not an important element. Because of its size and regional differences, and the historical shadow of slavery and the Civil War, the United States is radically divided over issues of war, taxes, welfare, race, religion, abortion, and sex.

These conflicts are not just about the best means to pursue generally accepted ends. They are about ultimate values. Yet they do not threaten the stability and legitimacy of the system. Except for a small lunatic fringe, citizens of the United States are prepared to accept the results of the political and legal process even when those results contravene some of their most fundamental convictions. Americans may vilify one another as bigoted religious fanatics or morally depraved atheists, racist reactionaries or crypto-totalitarian socialists, but they know they will not be put up against the wall if their party loses an election. That Americans can share a common political system with people whose views they despise, and try to fight out their disagreements legally through the pursuit of power under that system, shows that the cohesion of American society is stronger than its divisions.

This cohesion is possible only because of a general commitment to the principles of limited government embodied in the Constitution. Individuals and groups can be confident that they will be protected by the rule of law from the arbitrary exercise of governmental power, and that the way they conduct their lives will be largely exempt from collective control based on majority preferences. The precise definition of those limits is controversial, but no one doubts that they exist.

Their importance has been brought home to us again by the Bush administration's contempt for the rule of law and its attempts to evade the limits on executive power, under the color of a war on terror. The worst of these abuses, like torture and indefinite detention, have been mostly inflicted on foreigners, but surveillance increasingly threatens domestic rights of privacy. I am optimistic enough to believe that our society's attachment to constitutional limits will prevent the domestic abuses from going very far, but in the treatment of non-Americans, precisely because of their weak or nonexistent legal protection, ruthlessness has been taken to shameful lengths.

Domestically, Americans continue to be embroiled in virulent conflicts, largely between conservatives and progressives. They disagree about what, if anything, the state should do about economic, racial, and sexual inequality; about the separation of church and state; about sexual and reproductive freedom; and about what limits, if any, to put on the freedom of expression. Conservatives are more interested in enforcing moral standards on the community and protecting private property, and less interested in protecting personal liberty and reducing inequality; with progressives, it is the reverse.

Within the progressive camp there is a further issue about how some of these conflicts should be pursued. Should the argument be about "first-order principles"—fundamental beliefs about religion, abortion, and homosexuality, for example—or should it be about "second-order principles" concerning what kinds of first-order principles may be used to justify the exercise of political and legal power? The liberal strand of progressive thought, shaped by such thinkers as John Rawls,[1] holds, for example, that to defend a woman's right to terminate her pregnancy it is not necessary to prove that the Catholic position that the fetus is a person from the moment of conception is false. It is sufficient to show that, under our system of rights, the first-order principles embodied in Catholic doctrine cannot legitimately be used to constrain private choice. This argument could be accepted as a political principle of limited government even by those

---

1. See Rawls, *Political Liberalism* (New York: Columbia University Press, 1993; second edition, 1996).

who hold that abortion is always morally impermissible. The same issue arises about gay rights. In the liberal view, their defense need not depend on the argument that there is nothing wrong with homosexuality; it can be based instead on the narrower political principle that private sexual conduct should not fall under government control.

But another school of thought, which can be described as progressive but not liberal, holds that those who oppose conservative positions on such issues as abortion and homosexuality should engage directly with conservatives on the first-order moral and religious questions. Proponents of this view argue that in defending rights to abortion and to sexual freedom it is a political and philosophical mistake to rely on limits to the legitimate scope and grounds of collective control over the individual. Instead, they maintain, defenders of these rights should argue frankly that conservative religious views on sexual morality and abortion are false. Since that is what most liberals believe anyway, the claim not to be relying on it looks phony. Progressives should not devote their energies to defending individual rights against majority opinion. They should concentrate instead on changing majority opinion.

Michael Sandel, a professor of government at Harvard University, is a prominent contributor to this debate. He is a progressive who is opposed to contemporary liberalism. He believes that liberal appeals to individual rights and to the broad values of fairness and equality make a poor case for the progressive cause, both as a matter of strategy and as a matter of principle. The country and the Democratic Party would be better off, he thinks, if progressives made more of an effort to inspire the majority to adopt their vision of the common good and make it the democratic ground for public policy and law. In the introduction to his book, *Public Philosophy*,[2] Sandel writes: "Fairness isn't everything. It does not answer the hunger for a public life of larger meaning, because it does not connect the project of self-government with people's desire to participate in a common good greater than themselves." He goes on to argue:

> Liberals often worry that inviting moral and religious argument
> into the public square runs the risk of intolerance and coercion.
> The essays in this volume respond to that worry by showing that
> substantive moral discourse is not at odds with progressive public
> purposes, and that a pluralist society need not shrink from engaging
> the moral and religious convictions its citizens bring to public life.

2. Michael Sandel, *Public Philosophy: Essays on Morality in Politics* (Cambridge, Mass.: Harvard University Press, 2005).

In place of liberalism, Sandel endorses a "republican" tradition of self-government that he identifies with the earlier history of the United States. In contrast to the individualism that he claims is at the heart of liberal theory, republicanism, as he understands it, gives primacy to the communal aim of shared self-government, and what he calls "soulcraft," the cultivation of virtue in the citizenry by the design of political, social, and economic institutions. It gives personal morality a larger role in political life than liberalism does and in this respect tries to meet the moralism of the right on its own ground:

> The problems in the theory of procedural liberalism show up in the practice it inspires. A politics that brackets [i.e., that excludes from discussion] morality and religion too completely soon generates its own disenchantment. Where political discourse lacks moral resonance, the yearning for a public life of larger meaning finds undesirable expression. The Christian Coalition and similar groups seek to clothe the naked public square with narrow, intolerant moralisms. Fundamentalists rush in where liberals fear to tread.

Anyone concerned over the political success of conservatism in recent years must be interested in such a critique.

Public Philosophy is a collection of previously published essays and opinion pieces from the past twenty years, many of them only a few pages long but some quite substantial. Sandel's general approach is familiar from his previous books, *Liberalism and the Limits of Justice*[3] and *Democracy's Discontent*,[4] but he usefully summarizes his ideas here and applies them to a range of current issues.

[II]

Sandel's views on substantive issues of social welfare and personal liberty are not very different from those of most liberals. He supports affirmative action, gay rights, abortion rights, and stem cell research; opposes state lotteries and advertising in the classroom; and is doubtful about assisted suicide. In economic policy, he is a sentimentalist who thinks small is beautiful:

> Where the liberal regards the expansion of individual rights
> and entitlements as unqualified moral and political progress,
> the communitarian [a name for Sandel's position, which he will

---

3. Sandel, *Liberalism and the Limits of Justice* (Cambridge: Cambridge University Press, 1982).
4. Sandel, *Democracy's Discontent* (Cambridge, Mass.: Harvard University Press, 1996).

eventually reject; see below] is troubled by the tendency of liberal programs to displace politics from smaller forms of association to more comprehensive ones. Where libertarian liberals defend the private economy and egalitarian liberals defend the welfare state, communitarians worry about the concentration of power in both the corporate economy and the bureaucratic state, and the erosion of those intermediate forms of community that have at times sustained a more vital public life.

Such nostalgic rhetoric may suggest that Sandel is uneasy about Social Security and Medicare and would oppose a single-payer health care system as an extension of the faceless bureaucratic state. But so far as I know, he does not draw such conclusions.[5]

His theoretical differences with liberalism are more significant, and he has used this disagreement to define himself as a thinker. Unfortunately, his understanding of liberal political theory is defective, and his description of the principles and arguments of those he wants to criticize is persistently inaccurate—for example, his claim that a liberal couldn't have opposed slavery before the Civil War because it was too controversial. To evaluate Sandel's disagreement with the principles of contemporary liberalism, we have first to disentangle it from his faulty account of what those principles are.

The term "liberalism" applies to a wide range of political positions, from the libertarianism of economic laissez-faire to the democratic egalitarianism of the welfare state. In its European usage the term suggests the former rather than the latter; in American usage it is the reverse. But all liberal theories have this in common: They hold that the sovereign power of the state over the individual is bounded by a requirement that individuals remain inviolable in certain respects, and that they must be treated equally. The state is a human creation, and it is subject to moral constraints that limit the subordination of the individual to the collective will and the collective interest. Those constraints have to be embodied in political institutions. They include not only the familiar freedoms of religion, expression, association, and privacy but also equality of political status, equality before the law, and, in the welfare state version, equality of opportunity and fairness in the social and economic structure of the society.

---

5. One notable moralistic departure is his distaste for the free market, because of its reliance on self-interested motives rather than common purposes. This leads him to oppose a market in emissions permits, whereby countries or enterprises that pollute less can sell emission credits to those that pollute more. Sandel's complaint is that such a market fails to condemn the moral wrongness of pollution. This righteous view ignores the fact that there can be no economic activity without pollution, so it can hardly be wrong in itself. The point of tradeable emissions permits is simply to reduce the total burden of pollution most efficiently.

Liberal constraints on the exercise of collective power are therefore both negative and positive. The purely negative liberalism of Friedrich Hayek and Robert Nozick is unusual; most American liberals favor not just the protection of individual rights but a form of distributive justice that combats poverty and large inequalities perpetuated by inheritance and class. It is this form of egalitarian liberalism, particularly as represented by its leading theorist, John Rawls, that Sandel has spent his career opposing.

Sandel's point of attack is Rawls's central claim that individual rights and principles of social justice should take precedence over the broad advancement of human welfare by some standard of what constitutes the good life. Rawls's argument makes precise the familiar moral intuition that the end does not always justify the means, that there are principles of right—principles that govern how individuals should be treated by the state—that may not be violated on grounds of expediency. As Sandel writes:

> For Rawls, as for Kant, the right is prior to the good in two respects, and it is important to distinguish them. First, the right is prior to the good in the sense that certain individual rights "trump," or outweigh, considerations of the common good. Second, the right is prior to the good in that the principles of justice that specify our rights do not depend for their justification on any particular conception of the good life.

The distinction between these two kinds of priority is important because some liberals accept the priority of rights in practice (the first kind) but not in justification (the second kind). John Stuart Mill, for example, was a great defender of individual rights to freedom of expression and to other forms of liberty as a bar to the tyranny of the majority. But in contrast to Rawls, Mill justified those rights on the ground that protecting them strictly was the best way to serve the cause of general human happiness. As a utilitarian, Mill believed that the only way to justify a moral or political principle is to show that it will promote good lives, which to him meant happy lives.

While acknowledging the achievements of utilitarianism, Rawls argues that this derivation of rights and justice from a particular conception of the general welfare is morally mistaken. His main criticism of utilitarianism is that while the promotion of good overall outcomes is important, there is another type of moral requirement that underlies rights and social justice. This is the requirement that a society should treat its members as equals, and it explains directly why there are limits on the degree to which individuals can be subordinated to the collective interest, the general welfare, or the preferences of the majority. Equal treatment means protecting the equal rights of all members of a society, even if they belong to an unpopular minority, and refusing to allow any members to be excluded from social or economic opportunities or to fall below some decent minimum standard of living. Furthermore, since "the right," so understood, has a different moral foundation from the promotion of good overall outcomes, its principles can be identified without settling some of the major disagreements about the ultimate ends of life that divide the citizens of a typically pluralistic modern society.

Utilitarians have not been persuaded, and neither has Sandel. Sandel is not a utilitarian, since he believes in goods other than the sum of happiness, such as communal solidarity, strong family ties, and the search for higher meaning in our lives. But he agrees with utilitarians, in opposition to Rawls, that individual rights and principles of distributive justice are subordinate to the collective good, and have to be justified by reference to it: "Principles of justice depend for their justification on the moral worth or intrinsic good of the ends they serve."

The protection of religious or sexual freedom, or freedom of expression, depends, he believes, on whether those freedoms serve valuable ends. So he says protection should be extended to demonstrators against racism and segregation, but not to Nazi demonstrators. On that principle, those who regard homosexuality as sinful should be opposed to allowing a parade for gay rights. Sandel acknowledges that "On any theory of rights, certain general rules and doctrines are desirable to spare judges the need to recur to first principles in every case that comes before them." In other words, he might accept a fairly strict rule protecting political speech because it would be too time-consuming to decide in every case whether it was on balance beneficial or harmful. But he seems to think that if there are limits on censorship, they have no more fundamental justification than that.

As for freedom of religion, Sandel holds that it depends on the assumption "that religious belief, as characteristically practiced in a particular society, produces ways of being and acting that are worthy of honor and appreciation—either because they are admirable in themselves or because they foster qualities of character that make good citizens." So if someone believes that this is not true of most religions other than his own, or of atheism, he has no reason, according to Sandel's theory of rights, to support their toleration. He may in fact have an overwhelming reason to suppress heresy, since it puts other members of the society in spiritual danger. Sandel would presumably regard such a person's religious beliefs as mistaken, and he may even hold that the value of a religion doesn't depend on its truth. But he could not fault the opponent of religious liberty for failing to conform to Sandel's theory of rights or justice.

[III]

As these examples show, there is something paradoxical about liberalism, for it asks us on moral grounds to refrain from using the power of the state to enforce on others some of our most deeply held moral convictions about how people should conduct themselves—religiously, sexually, or expressively. This liberal restraint comes from our special moral relation to fellow members of our society—a collectivity that can coerce each of its members, but only if it claims to act in the name of all of them. Sandel's response, that there are no legitimate rights that cannot be derived from the good, and therefore no limits, in principle, on the use of political power to pursue the good as the majority sees it, is much simpler and easier to understand. It belongs to the enduring tradition of teleological theories, according to which all moral principles are just means to an end, whether it be happiness, salvation, or human perfection.

This disagreement runs through the history of moral philosophy, and will continue to do so. But when Sandel attempts to argue for his position, the result is deeply confused: Sandel finds Rawls's nonteleological liberalism so incomprehensible that he misinterprets it as a teleological theory with a very special conception of the good, based on a peculiar conception of the self, one that calls to mind Sartre's existentialism. This is the notion of "the unencumbered self, a self understood as prior to and independent of purposes and ends."

> The unencumbered self describes first of all the way we stand toward the things we have, or want, or seek. It means there is always a distinction between the values I *have* and the person I *am*. To identify any characteristics as *my* aims, ambitions, desires, and so on, is always to imply some subject "me" standing behind them, at a certain distance, and the shape of this "me" must be given prior to any of the aims or attributes I bear.... It rules out the possibility of what we might call *constitutive* ends. No role or commitment could define me so completely that I could not understand myself without it. No project could be so essential that turning away from it would call into question the person I am....
>
> Only if the self is prior to its ends can the right be prior to the good. Only if my identity is never tied to the aims and interests I may have at any moment can I think of myself as a free and independent agent, capable of choice.

In Sandel's view, then, liberalism depends on the assumption that no end is valuable unless it is freely chosen by a completely featureless self, an agent without ties, obligations, values, or commitments. From this he draws the political consequence that the liberal state must be a neutral framework of rights that refuses to choose among competing purposes and ends, leaving each individual free to pursue those ends on which his choice has conferred the only value it can have. Liberalism is therefore unable to make sense of the idea of the common good. Instead, it favors "a procedural republic, concerned less with cultivating virtue than with enabling persons to choose their own values."

To this caricature of Rawls and other liberals Sandel offers the following counterargument:

> Certain moral and political obligations that we commonly
> recognize—such as obligations of solidarity, for example, or
> religious duties—may claim us for reasons unrelated to choice.
> Such obligations are difficult to dismiss as merely confused, and
> yet difficult to account for if we understand ourselves as free and
> independent selves, unbound by moral ties we have not chosen.

I know of no liberal theorist who subscribes to the extreme freedom from moral ties that Sandel describes. It is totally inaccurate to attribute such a view to Rawls, whose argument in *A Theory of Justice* is explicitly based on the defining importance of religious commitments and family ties, and who regards communal solidarity and concern for a just version of the common good as fundamental requirements of justice.[6]

For Rawls, the requirement of limited political neutrality among religions or comparably ambitious secular ideals such as hedonism is based on the overwhelming importance and self-defining character of commitments and values that different members of a society may not share. It is precisely because we care so deeply, in ways we cannot change, about very different things, that it is so important to protect individual liberty and avoid the wholesale imposition of ultimate values. Evangelical Christians, atheistic libertines, and Buddhist monks do not have a common vision of the good life. Rawls sees the task of liberalism as that of upholding a form of solidarity and a conception of the common good that respects these differences. If we are going to treat as equals in a collective social enterprise those whose religious convictions we reject, we have to define the common good and the legitimate aims and applications of political control in a way that does not exclude them from the outset.

---

6. Sandel's repeated citations of the phrase "the self is prior to its ends" come from Rawls's argument against hedonism and other single-value teleological views, on the ground that there is a need in each life to combine and balance a plurality of ends and subject them to the moral constraints of the sense of justice. It has nothing to do with the idea of the "unencumbered self." See Rawls, *A Theory of Justice* (Cambridge, Mass.: Harvard University Press, 1971; revised edition, 1999), sections 84 and 85.

The alternative would be to allow the majority to use state power to promote the good of everyone as defined by their religion. But if I were part of such a majority, I would then be treating the minority in a way that I could not accept as politically legitimate if I were subjected to it myself—if, that is, my own unconditional religious commitments put me in the minority instead. My sense of justice and equal respect should therefore inhibit the blanket enforcement of my own views in ways that are not essential to the public pursuit of the common good. Taxes, military spending, and environmental policies have to be decided collectively. Religious observance doesn't—though it took a long time to realize this.

[IV]

Sandel's misunderstanding becomes particularly clear in his comments on abortion. Liberals propose to "bracket," or set aside, the question whether abortion is morally wrong, and to defend the legal right to abortion on the ground that women's liberty in a personal matter of this kind may not be overruled simply because of the religious convictions of the majority. Sandel's reply is that we can "bracket" the moral question only if we first determine that the Catholic position is false. He argues: "The more confident we are that fetuses are, in the relevant moral sense, different from babies, the more confident we can be in affirming a political conception of justice that sets aside the controversy about the moral status of fetuses." This is not a counterargument but a mere begging of the question: To use as a premise the falsity of the Catholic position on abortion is not to "bracket" the question but to answer it, so it cannot be a condition for setting it aside. Sandel has again interpreted the priority of right as being intelligible only if it serves the good.

In the longest essay in *Public Philosophy*, a review of Rawls's second book, *Political Liberalism*, Sandel seeks to discredit Rawls's aim of trying to set aside conflicts among conceptions of the good life in determining principles of justice by claiming that such a principle of neutrality would have favored Stephen Douglas's position in the debates with Lincoln over slavery. Because the free and slave states were so divided on the matter, Douglas advocated leaving the choice concerning the authorization of slavery to the individual states and territories, and avoiding a national decision. Sandel sees this as an example of the sort of liberal neutrality with respect to deeply contested moral issues that Rawls favors.

But the state is supposed to be neutral not about all contested moral questions, but only about those that do not have to be decided politically. Slavery, unlike religion or private sexual relations, was a public institution, part of the legal system of property. It carried profound implications for political representation and equality (according to the Three-Fifths Compromise of 1787, each slave counted as three-fifths of a person in both the distribution of taxes and the apportionment of seats in Congress). Slavery was part of the basic structure of American society, and had been a central issue of justice since the Revolution.

Insofar as Rawls favors state neutrality and limits to the enforcement of the majority's values, he does so only in regard to those questions concerning values that can be left to private choice, and that do not have to be answered collectively in order to reach important political decisions. This boundary is itself contested, but slavery was never regarded, either by its defenders or by its opponents, as a question of private, personal morality. The idea makes no sense, and Sandel's invocation of it shows how deeply he misunderstands the liberal position.[7]

He points out, as if it were an objection to liberalism, that moral disagreements about justice and rights are just as deep as disagreements about religion and sexual morality. But liberals have always known this. They claim only that there are some disagreements about the good life and ultimate values that we don't have to settle in order to decide collectively how we will pursue justice and the common good. This leaves plenty of disagreements that we do have to battle over, and that demand all our resources of solidarity and trust to settle peacefully.

[V]

Notwithstanding his misinterpretations of Rawls, Sandel's disagreement with liberalism is real and important. He denies that the right is prior to the good, and he opposes even the limited state neutrality about nonpolitical values that liberals favor. Nothing I have said so far proves that he is wrong.

In the flood of response that followed the publication of Rawls's *A Theory of Justice* in 1971, Sandel was grouped with Michael Walzer and Alasdair MacIntyre as a defender of "communitarianism," as opposed to individual rights, and their argument was called the communitarian critique of liberalism. Sandel doesn't like the term, and in this book he explains why it doesn't accurately describe his position:

> The term "communitarian" is misleading...insofar as it implies
> that rights should rest on the values or preferences that prevail in

---

7. It is true, as Sandel emphasizes, that religious arguments were invoked by abolitionists against slavery, but religious arguments were also used to defend slavery. The issue of political morality could not be legitimately settled by determining which of these positions was theologically correct.

any given community at any given time. Few, if any, of those who have challenged the priority of the right are communitarians in this sense. The question is not whether rights should be respected, but whether rights can be identified and justified in a way that does not presuppose any particular conception of the good.

Sandel rejects majoritarianism or the authority of community values:

> The mere fact that certain practices are sanctioned by the traditions of a particular community is not enough to make them just. To make justice the creature of convention is to deprive it of its critical character, even if allowance is made for competing interpretations of what the relevant tradition requires.

Instead, Sandel thinks justice and rights depend on what is actually good, and what rules or institutions serve those ends; he is not a relativist. So there is for him no substitute for moral argument and moral reasoning about what is truly valuable in determining the character of a just society.

He applies this principle most effectively in the essay "Moral Argument and Liberal Toleration: Abortion and Homosexuality." There he distinguishes between two styles of argument,

> The "naïve" and the "sophisticated." The naïve view holds that the justice of laws depends on the moral worth of the conduct they prohibit or protect. The sophisticated view holds that the justice of such laws depends not on a substantive moral judgment about the conduct at stake, but instead on a more general theory about the respective claims of majority rule and individual rights, of democracy on the one hand, and liberty on the other.

He prefers the naïve view and it is hard not to sympathize with him. He believes he can show that abortion is not wrong and that homosexuality is just as good as heterosexuality, and he is willing to stake the legal issue on those claims. As I have said, there is something paradoxical about the sophisticated, liberal alternative. Why should anyone, except for strategic reasons, want to defend the legal right to abortion and toleration for homosexuals in a way that someone who regards both practices as sinful can accept?[8]

---

8. The debate about homosexuality may have moved irrevocably from the sophisticated to the naïve level when the issue became not merely toleration but same-sex marriage. Antisodomy laws can be opposed by the sophisticated argument, but it is not possible to defend same-sex marriage without asking the state to take a position on the value of homosexual relationships. Since marriage is a public institution, this is a battle that cannot be avoided once the issue has been raised.

The answer depends on a certain understanding of the complexity of moral theory. This is a deep issue: Do all moral standards derive from a single principle, or are there different basic principles for different kinds of entities? Rawls believed that the moral standards for social and political institutions were not derived from the standards for personal life, or from a common principle that yielded them both. Rather, he thought that justice, which is the special virtue of social institutions like the state, depended on the distinctive moral character of the state itself, as an immensely powerful form of collective agency.

As citizens, we are subject to the will of the majority, coercively enforced. The extent of that control and the grounds on which it is exercised are what is at issue. Rawls believed that constitutional limitations and requirements should reflect the democratic ideal that each member ought to be able to regard the system as acting on his authority, even when he may disagree with particular decisions or policies. He believed that this required not only political equality and civil liberties but also strong measures to combat racial, sexual, and socio-economic inequality.

Sandel's alternative, the untrammeled pursuit of the good, means that the state is not governed by special moral standards because of its collective power. He thinks we should join together to decide on the true ends of life, and then use the power of the state to create virtue and give everyone's life a meaning as part of something larger than themselves. This will lead to liberal toleration if we accept Mill's conception of human good. Or if we accept what seems to be Sandel's ideal, it will lead to an unmaterialistic culture of closely knit communities and strong family ties. But it will lead to theocracy, fascism, or communism for those who accept alternative conceptions of the human good.

The question, finally, is whether there is a special moral requirement that applies to political institutions and that has enough force to inhibit the coercive enactment of more comprehensive ideals of the human good. Sandel is convinced that we cannot justifiably subordinate our deepest personal convictions about the ultimate good for humanity to a system of respect for individual rights. Rawls and other Kantian liberals think that respect for our fellow citizens provides the moral resource needed to justify the protection of rights, and that it defines the restricted political terrain on which we ought to argue about our common institutions.

I do not think the answer to this question is clear-cut. Even if the political morality of equal respect identifies a fundamental value, there may be other values that it is not powerful enough to contain. Sandel may be right that the strongest religious convictions about abortion are like that, as well as other dogmatic beliefs about the only path to salvation. In the face of certain conflicts, liberal restraint may be overwhelmed. But that does not mean it is without force.

Liberalism is a minority conviction in the world at large. To most people values are values, and political power should be used to implement them: What else is it for? But Sandel's ideal republic of comprehensive virtue would abandon a form of civic respect that has been of inestimable value, and threaten one of the indispensable grounds of political stability in our free, stormy, magnificently diverse nation. To use a phrase of Jürgen Habermas, constitutional patriotism should be enough to satisfy what Sandel calls our "hunger for a public life of larger meaning." A hunger that demands more from the state will lead us where history has shown we should not want to go.

IO

MacKinnon on Sexual Domination

Catharine MacKinnon, the author of *Women's Lives, Men's Laws*,[1] is an emblematic figure in American life and law. For many years she and her late collaborator, Andrea Dworkin, were the standardbearers of antiliberal feminism, and as a lawyer, writer, and teacher, she has had an explosive impact. She comes from the Left, and her antiliberalism, like the antiliberalism of Marx, derides individual rights as an ideological mask for the protection of existing structures of domination. In Marx's case, the targets were rights of private property and due process, instruments of class domination. In MacKinnon's case, they are freedom of speech and the right to privacy, and the domination they uphold is sexual. Her career has been dedicated to attacking male dominance, not as a denial of individual rights to women, but as a deep systemic inequality that defines the difference between the sexes and the meaning of sex. And she has made U.S. antidiscrimination law her weapon: "In societies governed by the rule of law, law is typically a status quo instrument; it does not usually guarantee rights that society is predicated on denying. In this context equality law is unusual: social equality does not exist, yet a legal guarantee of equality does."

Unlike liberal advocates of equality for women, who concentrate on securing equal opportunity in employment and education, equal

1. Catharine MacKinnon, *Women's Lives, Men's Laws* (Cambridge, Mass.: Harvard University Press, 2005).

pay, maternity benefits, free day care, and other measures in order to close the social and economic gap between men and women, MacKinnon is interested primarily in sex. Her subjects are rape, pornography, prostitution, and sexual harassment. (She shares the liberal concern over abortion, but with an interesting twist; see below.) Her view is that the sexual domination of women is the heart of sexual inequality, and that it underlies the familiar public inequalities. Nothing will really change unless it is attacked directly:

> Sexuality, as socially organized, is deeply misogynistic. To male dominance, of which liberalism is the current ruling ideology, the sexual misogyny that is fundamental to all these problems cannot be seen as a sex equality issue because its sexuality is premised on sex *in*equality. Equality law cannot apply to sexuality because equality is not sexy and inequality is.

There is not much romance in her view of the erotic life: "Women are commonly raped, battered, sexually harassed, sexually abused as children, forced into motherhood and prostitution, depersonalized, denigrated, and objectified—then told this is fun and equal by the left and just and natural by the right."

Women's Lives, Men's Laws is a diverse collection of MacKinnon's writings and speeches from the past twenty-five years. It is repetitious: A cultural icon inevitably says the same things to many audiences. It also seethes with loathing for her enemies such as the American Civil Liberties Union, described as the center of the "pro-pimp lobby." But the book contains much that is impressive, both intellectually and rhetorically, and it is instructive both about the history of MacKinnon's battles and about the issues. Particularly valuable is a long essay originally published in the *Yale Law Journal*, "Reflections on Sex Equality under Law," which sets out her position clearly and incisively. She believes that the sexual inequality of American society can be legally assailed by appealing to the constitutional bar against group subordination that developed out of the country's long struggle with slavery and racism. But sex is not like race: equality cannot mean merely that women should be treated exactly as men are treated, since that standard would be met if both men and women were denied pregnancy leave and the right to have an abortion. (This, as she says, is the equality that prohibits both the rich and the poor from sleeping under the bridges of Paris.)

MacKinnon's originality is to have extended the reach of this familiar point far beyond the biological, by linking it to her visceral sense of the omnipresent sexual and personal subordination of women. Explicit legal and economic discrimination and the unequal impact of formally neutral laws are only the tip of the iceberg, and therefore the legal attack must cut much deeper than in the case of racial inequality. It must invade sexual life itself. And the means of attack should be not the criminal law, whose enforcement is too easily neglected by male authorities when it threatens male domination, but the civil law, which permits injured women and their lawyers to initiate action and claim redress. It also, though she doesn't mention it, imposes a lower burden of proof.

MacKinnon's greatest success has been in the development of sexual harassment law, which, as she explains in a detailed account, grew from a series of cases, some of which she argued, based on the Civil Rights Act of 1964. The Act prohibited discrimination in employment on the basis of sex as well as race. Twelve years later, a woman who was fired after refusing her supervisor's sexual advances successfully sued for discrimination under this provision. The concept of sexual harassment was subsequently extended through other cases to include persistent unwanted sexual attention, sexually charged hostility, and perhaps individual gross performances like the one of which Paula Jones accused Bill Clinton. MacKinnon explains why this expansion of the idea of discrimination was both correct and important. These are not just injuries to an individual who happens to be a woman: She is subjected to them because she is a woman, since women are conventionally regarded as fair game for such treatment in our civilization, whereas men are not.

The reference to group subordination in identifying a legally actionable injury to the individual is the linchpin of MacKinnon's conception of equality. She has no use for purely individual rights, much less universal ones. The point is to fight domination. This leads her to a distinctive and significant position on abortion, which she thinks should be defended on grounds not of privacy or bodily autonomy, but of equality: "If sex equality existed socially—if women were recognized as persons, sexual aggression were truly deviant, and childrearing were shared and consistent with a full life rather than at odds with it—the fetus still might not be considered a person but the question of its political status would be a very different one." But as things are, "abortion provides a window of relief in an unequal situation from which there is no exit. Until this context changes, only the pregnant woman can choose life for the unborn."

MacKinnon condemns privacy as a value that has traditionally allowed men to get away with anything, under a code of mutual protection. In some respects her wishes have come true, and she celebrates the exposure of powerful males like Clinton and Clarence Thomas. But her attempts to extend the civil rights technique beyond sexual harassment in two further directions have failed—one regrettably and the other fortunately. The former, a federal Violence against Women Act that she helped draft, would have permitted women to bring civil suits where states failed to provide adequate protection. It was passed by Congress but struck down by the Supreme Court in 2000, on the ground that it violated the division of authority between the states and the federal government—an unusual example of heightened federalism, which MacKinnon criticizes in a trenchant essay originally published in the *Harvard Law Review*.

The other instance, MacKinnon and Dworkin's most famous exploit, was the attempt to make pornography civilly actionable as a form of sex discrimination. The creators and distributors of pornography would be subject to suit by women used in its production, women assaulted as a result of men's consumption of it, or women whose subordination is caused by the general traffic in pornography. This was rightly seen as a thinly veiled form of privatized censorship. In the version adopted by the city of Indianapolis, it was struck down by the federal courts in 1984 as a violation of freedom of speech. Liberals opposed it solidly, and a group called the Feminist Anti-Censorship Task Force (FACT) filed an amicus curiae brief, earning MacKinnon's special rage.

Her insistence on breaking down the liberal barriers of privacy and freedom of expression in order to exercise state control over sexual life can make MacKinnon look similar in motivation to the moralistic right, but she rejects the charge. In an essay called "Beyond Moralism: Directions in Sexual Harassment Law," she argues effectively that the objection to sexual harassment derives none of its force from sexual puritanism and is addressed solely to the unequal treatment of women. But in the case of the pornography ordinance, her insistence that this is not moralistic content-based censorship rings hollow. I don't mean that she is a puritan, but her attitude to pornography and its consumers is massively moralistic. That men enjoy seeing women in these scenarios is itself what she hates. The feeble psychological experiments she cites, and the anecdotes about pornography being used as a guide in sexual assaults, are merely efforts to lend the weight of interpersonal harm to an essentially moral revulsion toward a form of male sexual pleasure by which she feels violated.

I do not have, as she has from her legal work, firsthand knowledge of the depths of female oppression, but I have every reason to accept her grim assurance that the lives of many women are filled from childhood with degradation, rape, violence, and coercion. I share her belief that many men fear and despise women. But the idea that pornography bears a significant causal responsibility for all this is remarkably unimaginative and is not supported, so far as I know, by evidence that sexual violence increases when pornography becomes more available in a society. Some of the most misogynistic and abusive cultures are those with the strictest censorship, and some of the least misogynistic, such as Sweden, were the first to lift restrictions.

MacKinnon is right to insist that the unequal status of women pervades sexuality and is not limited to the public sphere. But this causes her to undervalue sexual pleasure, which we all have to take where we can find it. The huge pornography industry serves this end by feeding people's fantasies. Since she finds most male fantasies revolting and degrading to women, and most consumers of pornography are men, this doesn't matter to her. In fact she wants to stop it, and therefore fixes on the illusion that she can fight inequality by controlling men's fantasy life.

What about female sexual pleasure? MacKinnon mentions it only once, in a riposte to Judge Richard Posner's unwise claim that men have a stronger sex drive than women. This, she says ignores "the clitoral orgasm, which, once it gets going, goes on for weeks, and no man can keep up with it, to no end of the frustration of some. (This underlies the often nasty edge to the query 'Did you come?' when it means, 'Aren't you done yet? I am.')" We are evidently in a war zone.

MacKinnon's antiliberal credo needs to be addressed seriously. It seems to me to require a moral justification that she does not even attempt to provide. It is not enough, in arguing for the deployment of state power, to point to deep social inequalities and say that this is a way to attack them. Not only do the means have to be effective, but they have to respect limits on legitimate invasion by the state of the personal autonomy of each of its citizens. This too is a requirement of equal treatment, though it is individualistically defined. If it is given no weight and automatically overridden by claims of group inequality and group subordination, we will get tyranny in the name of equality—a familiar result. MacKinnon should either explain why her contempt for rights of privacy, autonomy, and freedom of expression does not have this consequence, or else explain why it is acceptable.

PART III

Humanity

II

Williams: The Value of Truth

The virtuoso blend of analytic philosophy, classical scholarship, historical consciousness, and uninhibited curiosity marks *Truth and Truthfulness*[1] unmistakably as a work by Bernard Williams. He responds to Rousseau and Diderot; Thucydides, Herodotus, and Homer; Nietzsche, Hume, Plato, and Kant; Rorty, Habermas, and Hayden White. He manages to be frequently entertaining, and never to show off.

The book is about what Williams calls the "virtues" of truth—that is, the value we attach to certain relations or attitudes to the truth, notably accuracy and sincerity, and including the modern virtue of authenticity. The book is also, more indirectly, a response to skeptics about the reality or intelligibility of truth—the "deniers," as he calls them—and he leans over backward to find something other than confusion in their position, or in its underlying motives. Recent skeptics about truth have laid themselves open to easy rebuttal by overgeneralizing their doubts into a denial that there is such a thing as truth, or that it matters. Nobody really believes this, says Williams, including the deniers themselves. There are plenty of plain everyday truths—that today is Wednesday, that plants need water, that Paris is the capital of France—and no possessor of language can seriously think otherwise. "But," says Williams, "there may well be much of

1. Bernard Williams, *Truth and Truthfulness: An Essay in Genealogy* (Princeton, N.J.: Princeton University Press, 2002).

the critique that the reply leaves untouched: the suspicions about historical narrative, about social representations, about self-understanding, about psychological and political interpretation—all of this may remain as worrying as the deniers suggest."

Williams thinks that it is important to address these worries because he believes that the alienation of the humanistic academic left, with its rhetoric of power as the ruling standard in place of truth, is destructive of the only authority that the academy can hope to claim, an authority based on accuracy and honesty. And he believes we cannot understand those virtues apart from a belief in the reality and importance of truth.

His approach is unorthodox. Unlike most philosophers of the analytic tradition, he has not kept himself aloof from the rest of the humanities, and he wishes to address the skeptics in other fields in terms that will make sense to them. In particular, he objects to the strongly ahistorical character of analytic philosophy: the amount it tries to accomplish by conceptual analysis and a priori argument alone. This book exemplifies Williams's conviction that philosophy must use history, including historical imagination, to understand and defend values of any kind.

The question that Williams raises is easy to overlook: Why should we care about truth and truthfulness in the way we do? It is easy to overlook because there seems to be a simple instrumental answer: The truth is extremely useful, whether it is about the strength of building materials, or the safety of a food additive, or the intentions of someone with whom you are making a contract. Your life depends on most of your beliefs being true, and it therefore depends on a cultural norm of accuracy in the formation of beliefs and in their transmission.

Still, the functional utility of such a norm does not explain the value we assign to truth and truthfulness for their own sake. By and large, we think it is good to believe and to tell the truth whether this is instrumentally useful or not. Most of us are not at all comforted by the thought that what we don't know won't hurt us. In fact, the norm would not possess even its instrumental value unless most people also valued it intrinsically. As Williams remarks, "The reason why useful consequences have flowed from people's insistence that their beliefs should be true is surely, a lot of the time, that their insistence did not look just to those consequences but rather toward the truth: that it was bloody-minded rather than benefit-minded."

This is a common feature of ethical norms, from promise-keeping to property rights to the rule of law. Their social usefulness is not enough to explain the individual motivation to adhere to them, and without this distinctive individual attachment they would not be able to function as they do. The utility of promises depends on most people's unwillingness to break them even for reasons of utility. What kind of sense can we make of this?

Williams does not wish to answer the question by appealing to an abstract universal principle such as Kant's categorical imperative, which says essentially that you should not make an exception for yourself from rules that you would like everyone else to follow. He proposes instead to offer a historical account of how our specific attachment to the virtues of truth could have arisen, naturally but contingently—an account that will allow us to understand who we are and to affirm our values without further justification.

This is what he means by calling the book "an essay in genealogy." The term is an explicit reference to Nietzsche's *Genealogy of Morals*. Williams wants to make our present attitudes to truth intelligible through a historical interpretation, but one that explains how they have gone beyond their historical sources. It will be a partly functional explanation of dispositions that do not have a purely functional value. It will not reduce the value of truth to that of some end that truth serves, but will try to make the value intelligible and "stable under reflection" by showing how in its modern form it has come to be associated with other values that we care about.

So the aim is very different from that of Nietzsche's most famous essay in genealogy. Nietzsche attempted to debunk Christian morality by finding its roots in hatred and resentment, whereas Williams proposes to offer what he calls a "vindicatory" genealogy of the virtues of truth—one that will reinforce rather than undermine our attachment to those virtues, while at the same time acknowledging their contingency.

As a classic example of vindicatory genealogy Williams cites Hume's account of the origin of what he called the "artificial virtue" of justice: respect for property rights and the obligation of contracts. According to Hume, these values arose because the rules of property and contract are vital improvements in the condition of human life, but they survive because people brought up under those conventions come to be attached to them for their own sake, so that a failure of rectitude damages their self-esteem and forfeits the respect of others.

In spite of occasional remarks that are seized on by the deniers to claim him as an ally, Nietzsche was not a skeptic about the reality or value of truth. Indeed, he thought that the capacity to face the truth and avoid illusion, particularly about oneself, was all-important, though difficult and not conducive to happiness. Williams thinks of himself as pursuing a Nietzschean project of "revaluation" of the values of truth through self-understanding. It is a revaluation because it starts over, from a contingent historical perspective, in order to find out whether it is possible to regain confidence in values that have lost their hope of universal validation through a religious or metaphysical world picture or through the exercise of pure reason.

Williams wants to vindicate these values without making what he regards as excessive claims of universality or necessity; he is a deep-dyed anti-Platonist, and particularly in ethics he is an opponent of the transcendental ambition, typified also by Kant, of trying to ground our values in something higher than the contingencies of human history and psychology. This is a major element in Williams's earlier writings, such as his *Ethics and the Limits of Philosophy* (1985). Disdain for high-mindedness is one of his signatures. It may be possible to reaffirm the virtues of truth and the modern culture of political liberalism in which those virtues are embedded, but he believes that to reinstate this confidence in the absence of a transcendental validation, we need history.

The history that Williams offers is partly fictional. This belongs to an old philosophical tradition, found particularly in political philosophy, called "state of nature theory"—a tradition that includes the famous fiction of the social contract. Hobbes, or Locke, or Rousseau imagines how political institutions and their governing principles might have arisen by agreement out of a more primitive condition of life to meet human needs that could not be met without them, and how human beings would have to change to allow those institutions to be stable. It is a way of connecting a moral structure with more basic features of human nature, human psychology, and the human condition, so that the structure can be seen as a development within the natural order—but one that is cultural and not merely sociobiological.

Williams conceives state of nature theory as a form of ethical naturalism: "explaining the ethical in terms of an account of human beings which is to the greatest possible extent prior to ideas of the ethical." He proposes to apply this technique to the virtues of truth—sincerity and accuracy—by starting out from an imaginary preliterate state of nature (not to be identified, he says, with the Pleistocene) and then, as the story progresses, gradually folding into it some real history that will allow us to understand more fully where we are today with respect to truth in science, in politics, in history, in personal relations, and in individual self-awareness. By understanding how we arrived or might have arrived at those values, Williams thinks, we can help endow them with stability.

This seems to me a very strange project. To display our present values as the product of a possible or actual process of contingent development cannot vindicate them unless it shows that we have arrived at the right place. If our values would not be acceptable without this story, they are not acceptable with it, and if they are acceptable with it, they ought to be acceptable without it. The history may be interesting and even true, but how can it produce stability unless it helps us to appreciate justifications that can be used in the present—as social contract theories typically try to do? Vindication by history seems no more promising with regard to the virtues of truth than it does in politics.

It is because he rejects the universal ambitions of most moral philosophy that Williams is drawn to this alternative. He insists, for example, that the emergence of liberalism, with its commitment to toleration, liberty, and certain forms of equality, cannot be understood as a cognitive achievement—a discovery that this system of values is closer to being correct than its predecessors. But why, by contrast, should a history of how we came to be who we are serve as a source of confidence if the values we have ended up with do not sustain themselves? There are no doubt many submoral values that do not claim universality, and that can be understood only through the history of contingent local practices and customs. But the virtues of truth do not seem remotely like that.

This, I know, is the response of a hopeless Kantian, or even Platonist. Fortunately, much of what Williams has to offer can be detached from the state-of-nature framework, which is in any case submerged much of the time. The nonfictional history is more interesting, and serves as a backdrop for reflections on contemporary culture and a useful reminder of how much worse off we could be.

Williams observes first that the mere existence of language, with its central use to assert what is the case and to represent the speaker's beliefs, does not by itself provide an individual speaker with any reason not to lie if he can gain something by it, nor does it tell him how much trouble he should take to see that his beliefs are true. Further, as we have already noted, the fact that accuracy and sincerity have a collective utility does not explain why we should regard them as intrinsically valuable—yet without this attitude even their collective utility would not be sustainable.

When he sets out to paint trustworthiness in colors that make it intrinsically attractive, Williams does not rely on genealogy but simply talks about what the disposition is. It cannot be captured by a simple rule against lying, because it is sometimes perfectly all right to lie (particularly to someone who does not deserve the truth, such as the man bent on homicide), and because the distinction between lying outright and saying something literally true but deliberately misleading is less morally significant than it is sometimes taken to be. (Thus Williams opposes the "fetishizing of assertion," familiar from Catholic casuistry and illustrated by the story of Saint Athanasius, who, when asked by his pursuers, "Where is the traitor Athanasius?" replied, "Not far away!") Williams makes it intelligible why failure of trustworthiness in the more complex modern form should be a reason for shame, and for loss of respect from those whom we ourselves respect.

Williams explains why accuracy and the resistance to self-deception cannot be understood apart from truth—the way the world is, independent of our will. Thus, although wishful thinking threatens accuracy, the motivation of scientists by the desire for fame and glory does not threaten accuracy, because it does not abandon the principle that reality is resistant to our will. Williams is excellent on why the virtue of accuracy is a form of mental freedom, and on the awfulness of the kind of exercise of power, illustrated in Orwell's *1984*, that forces the abandonment of the ideal of truth by subordinating belief to the will of another instead of to reality.

In fact, the opposition between the virtues of truth and the pure exercise of power is very effectively brought out by Williams: "The victim recognizes the barefaced lie as a pure and direct exercise of power over him...and this is an archetypal cause of resentment: not just disappointment and rage, but humiliation and the recognition that in the most literal sense he has been made a fool of." Accuracy and trustworthiness represent a kind of equality in the relations between people, whereby each of them is subject not to the unanswerable will of others, but only to the stubborn independence of reality.

In politics, this expresses itself in a critical method that undermines many claims to legitimate domination: "If one comes to know that the sole reason one accepts some moral claim is that somebody's power has brought it about that one accepts it, when, further, it is in their interest that one should accept it, one will have no reason to go on accepting it." Williams says this "is one of liberalism's most powerful weapons, because it does not depend on merely asserting liberalism's own set of values against a rival set but mobilizes the values of truth in a distinctive political interest." It is an advantage, from Williams's point of view, that "although it does not rely on a theory of moral truth, it does deploy a theory of error." But here again I would ask how there can be a theory of error unless we assume that there is such a thing as truth in the vicinity, even if we aren't sure how to find it. What is error if not something that leads you away from the right answer?

In spite of the link between the virtues of truth and liberal political institutions, Williams doesn't believe that the truth is most likely to emerge from the free marketplace of ideas. The most effective truth-seeking communities, such as universities and scientific research establishments, exercise strict entry controls and do not give a hearing to every crank who thinks that he has something to say. The political protection of free expression is designed not to reach the truth but to guard against tyranny, with all its familiar horrors. It is those with a monopoly of the use of force who must be denied the right to restrict dissent. This is what Judith Shklar called the "liberalism of fear," and while it is only part of the justification for political freedom, it is the most basic part.

Williams's book is packed with interesting readings: for example, a discussion in the line of Lionel Trilling of how the modern conception of authenticity arose from a version found in Diderot, involving self-discovery and self-construction as an essentially social activity, rather than the version found in Rousseau, which depends merely on individual self-knowledge plus candor. Two of Williams's ten chapters are explicitly about history and historical truth. One ascribes to Thucydides the invention of historical time, in the sense of a single sequence of yesterdays in which anything that really happened must be located. Everything else is either false or a myth. By contrast, Williams contends (using Herodotus as his example), before Thucydides the past was regarded as partly indeterminate; it included legendary events without specific temporal location—where this did not mean merely that their precise location was not known. They were just thought of as having occurred "in legendary times," and the correct version of these events was to be determined not by historical evidence but by narrative tradition. Williams says that because Herodotus did not have the objective conception of linear historical time that Thucydides invented, this cannot be regarded as a confusion. This seems to me unnecessarily generous—another questionable subordination of philosophy to history—but be that as it may, the discussion, which engages with many learned commentators on the issue, is an extraordinary display of subtlety and imagination.

Williams's final chapter takes up familiar problems of the role of interpretation in history and its relation to truth. It argues sensibly that although history must start with plain facts of the kind that positivists like, and the generally available forms of explanation that apply at all times, this is both too much and too little for history. History requires a radical selection from among the bare facts, and their interpretation. Interests determine the value of an interpretation because they determine the questions that it needs to address. And yet the relativity of interpretation to interests does not mean that it is all a matter of choice: We cannot choose what makes sense of the past, any more than we can choose what is factually true. History is not like myth, which must meet only the standard of what a select audience would like to hear. But the fact that there continues to be a lively demand for myths about the past by many audiences makes the discipline of truth and objectivity in history indispensable.

It is particularly important, says Williams, for the survival of liberalism. "This claim may seem a joke, granted the raft of myth that has sustained liberal societies in the past and still helps to do so," he observes. "But it is truthful inquiry that has taken those myths to pieces.... Liberalism may have destroyed in some part its distinctive supporting stories about itself...but the resources of the liberalism of fear, which work everywhere, may keep it afloat. A truthful history will remind one of those resources, and of what it costs in terms of quite basic human loss if a mythical order takes over." Near the beginning of his book, Williams writes that "the most significant question is not about the truth-status of political or moral outlooks themselves. It is about the importance that those outlooks attach to other kinds of truth, and to truthfulness." This is a false contrast. The need to justify our moral and political convictions by something more than tradition cannot be separated from the aim of getting them right, and that is an indispensable part of what it is to care about the truth. But even if one doesn't heed Williams's call to give up the quest for moral truth in favor of genealogical vindication, a great deal of what he says about the moral importance of nonmoral truth remains true and vitally important.

12

Williams: Philosophy and Humanity

Bernard Williams brought philosophical reflection to an opulent array of subjects, with more imagination and with greater cultural and historical understanding than anyone else of his time. Three posthumously published collections of essays provide an overwhelming reminder of his incandescent and all-consuming intelligence. *The Sense of the Past*[1] was largely planned by Williams himself before his death in 2003; *In the Beginning Was the Deed*[2] treats topics he would have addressed more systematically in the book on political philosophy he planned but did not live to write; *Philosophy as a Humanistic Discipline*[3] brings together the most important essays not collected elsewhere, including the fullest statement of Williams's conception of philosophy, of its purpose, and of its relations to science, to history, and to human life.

In each of the collections there are some slight pieces, and also some overlap, but all three are marvelous books. While they range over many topics, they are held together by Williams's acute sense of historical contingency and his resistance to the aspiration of so much

1. Bernard Williams, *The Sense of the Past: Essays in the History of Philosophy*, edited with an introduction by Myles Burnyeat (Princeton, N.J.: Princeton University Press, 2006).

2. Bernard Williams, *In the Beginning Was the Deed: Realism and Moralism in Political Argument*, selected, edited, and with an introduction by Geoffrey Hawthorn (Princeton, N.J.: Princeton University Press, 2005).

3. Bernard Williams, *Philosophy as a Humanistic Discipline*, selected, edited, and with an introduction by A. W. Moore (Princeton, N.J.: Princeton University Press, 2006).

philosophy to be timeless. This project, of pulling philosophy, particularly moral philosophy, down from the stratosphere and resisting its most universal theoretical ambitions, is what has set Williams against the general grain and given rise to the strong responses to his work. He was the foremost representative in our day of the view that philosophical reflection of the highest rational order need not lead to transcendence of the more contingent features of human life. He believed that instead of trying to view ourselves with maximal detachment, from the point of view of the universe, we can obtain a more illuminating form of reflective distance from our concepts and values through historical self-consciousness, which is an immersion in contingency.

The history of philosophy itself is one part of this enterprise, and in Williams's hands it becomes a subtle appreciation of ideas that may be fundamentally unlike anything we could think now, but that also help us to understand our own ideas better. Two of his best books were on historical subjects: *Descartes: The Project of Pure Inquiry* (1978) and *Shame and Necessity* (1993), a profound study of Greek concepts of responsibility and luck that draws on literary, legal, and historical sources, as well as philosophy. He also developed, in later years, an absorbing interest in and admiration for Nietzsche, whose philosophical method of historical self-interpretation he more or less adopted.

Yet he always retained an unsurpassed admiration for Plato, whose "discontent with the finite" and hope that philosophy can lift us to a pure and timeless reality represents the polar opposite view. Williams loved Plato both for his powerful expression of the transcendent impulse that must be resisted and for his understanding, so vividly expressed in the dialogues, of points of view opposed to his own. Seven of the essays in *The Sense of the Past* are about Plato and Socrates, including "Plato: The Invention of Philosophy," a superb tribute to this magical, protean, essentially unacademic figure. Williams says:

> Plato was recognizably, I think, one of those creative thinkers and artists—it is not true of all, including some of the greatest—who are an immensely rich source of thoughts and images, too many, perhaps, for them all to have their place and use.... We should not think of him as constantly keeping his accounts, anxious of how his system will look in the history of philosophy.

So Williams denies that there is such a thing as "the theory of forms." But there is much tough and complex philosophy in Plato, and Williams provides penetrating analyses of Platonic discussions of justice, of knowledge and perception, of intrinsic goodness, and of the "immoralism" of Thrasymachus in the *Republic* and Callicles in the *Gorgias*.

Williams is much less drawn to Aristotle, who he says invented scholasticism and is therefore unique among great philosophers in deserving the more tedious parts of his legacy. But *The Sense of the Past* offers some fine discussions of Aristotle's doctrines, especially "Justice as a Virtue," which brilliantly exposes the error of trying to link the vice of injustice to the special motive of greed, and "Hylomorphism," which provides a critical but sympathetic understanding of Aristotle on the relation between mind and body. There are also interesting essays on Descartes, Nietzsche, Collingwood, and others—including a wonderful discussion of Descartes' *Meditations* as a work of fiction, whose first-person narrator, describing his process of thought over a succession of days, cannot be identified with Descartes, the author, who of course knows the outcome in advance. Williams comments:

> This might have been a work in which the thinker's fictional ignorance of how his reflections would turn out was convincingly sustained. To some extent it is so, and to that extent, one of the gifts offered to the reader by this extraordinary work is a freedom to write it differently, to set out with the thinker and end up in a different place. The rewriting of Descartes' story in that way has constituted a good deal of modern philosophy.

Williams insists on the importance of history in making the strange familiar and the familiar strange. An example is this comment on slavery and modern economic inequality:

> The standard Greek attitude to slavery was not that it was a just institution; nor, again, that it was an unjust institution....Their view rather was that the institution was necessary, and that for those subjected to it it was bad luck. In that sense, it lay outside the considerations of justice.
>
> For us it does not lie outside those considerations, and is a paradigm of injustice. However, this does not mean that those same traditional materials, economic or cultural necessity and bad luck, make no contribution to our thinking about social life. We use them all the time. It may be that we have the aspiration that no social or economic relation should lie outside considerations of justice. To the extent that we have that aspiration, we try either (with the Left) to replace necessity and luck with justice, or (with the Right) to show that the results of necessity and luck can be just. Neither project is such a success as to enable us to say that in these matters we have decisively gone beyond the ethical condition of the ancients.

An old saw has it that all politics is local. Williams believed that political theory, too, should be in a sense local, rather than universal, because it must be addressed to individuals in a particular place and time, and must offer them a justification for the exercise of political power that has persuasive force in light of standards that are accessible to them.

Williams believed that the distinction between illegitimate and legitimate states depends on whether their exercise of power over their subjects is sheer coercion or not. But whether a society can meet this "Basic Legitimation Demand" depends on whether its justification for the exercise of power will be morally persuasive in that historical situation. The requirement cannot be for justification sub specie aeternitatis. What is legitimate at one time may not be at another. This is the meaning of Williams's title, "In the Beginning Was the Deed," taken from Goethe's *Faust*: "No political theory can determine by itself its own application. The conditions in which the theory or any given interpretation of it makes sense to intelligent people are determined by an opaque aggregation of many actions and forces."

For example, even if liberal institutions and equal rights for women are necessary conditions of legitimacy for us now, this has not always been true. Justifications have to come to an end within the point of view of those to whom justification must be offered. There is no point, Williams says, in imagining oneself as "Kant at the court of King Arthur," judging its institutions from a universal standpoint.

This is the "relativism of distance" that Williams put forward in *Ethics and the Limits of Philosophy* (1985). It is one of his most controversial claims, and goes together with the thesis that reasons for action in general must start from something in the agent's subjective motivational set—that they must, in Williams's terms, be "internal" rather than "external" reasons. The search for truth about reasons for action, personal ethics, and political morality cannot aspire to the kind of objective validity that is a reasonable aim for science and mathematics. Williams claims that ethics is irreducibly perspectival, and that the perspective is local—not a universal human perspective.

In "Values, Reasons, and the Theory of Persuasion," one of the essays in *Philosophy as a Humanistic Discipline*, Williams observes that the internalist account of reasons does not by itself rule out the Kantian conclusion that every rational agent is implicitly committed to impartiality, and to its moral and political consequences. But he doesn't think that either Kant or anyone else has offered a persuasive argument for that conclusion, starting from inside some motivational structure shared by all rational beings. Those who disagree may appeal to the force of moral arguments themselves as revealing that motivational structure. But Williams would reply that, even if we find the moral reasons for impartiality compelling, that does not show that they appeal to reason as such, as opposed to something more local about us. This is one of the most fundamental disagreements in ethics.

A similar disagreement applies in political theory. While recognizing that it is possible to create stable and effective institutions only with the social and human material available at any given place and time, a modern liberal may still think we are advancing in a positive direction, overcoming moral mistakes of the past, as future ages may overcome our mistakes. But Williams says that liberalism has no theory of error, comparable to that which allows us to speak of progress in the history of science. He ridicules the idea that "if a morality is correct, it must apply to all those past people who were not liberals: they ought to have been liberals, and since they were not, they were bad, or stupid, or something on those lines."

That would certainly be an unreasonable theory of error. But one can believe in moral progress without accusing past ages of wickedness or stupidity (though there is plenty of both in all ages). Perhaps progress can occur only through a series of historical stages, in morality as in science. It is not because he was stupid that Thomas Aquinas was not a liberal, any more than it was stupidity that prevented Newton from discovering the theory of relativity—not to make more of the analogy than that.

Precisely because he is convinced that it is not a judgment from an absolute point of view, Williams sees no conflict between, for example, our confidence in the requirement of equal rights for all citizens and the refusal to judge that hierarchical societies in the past were unjust. Confidence need not be undermined by historical self-awareness. And he shrewdly adds:

> That does not mean, as Richard Rorty likes to suggest, that we
> must slide into a position of irony, holding to liberalism as practical
> liberals, but backing away from it as reflective critics. That posture
> is itself still under the shadow of universalism: it suggests that you
> cannot really believe in liberalism unless you hold it true in a sense
> which means that it applies to everyone.

Resistance to the external standpoint has a central part in Williams's rejection of utilitarianism, but he also thinks it tells against the possibility of ethical theory as such—if we understand by that a general theoretical explanation of the content of morality. He argues that what is fundamental in the ethical life are dispositions to act and feel in certain ways—dispositions to honesty and fidelity, for instance—and that these can exist only if truthfulness and keeping your word are valued in themselves, not merely as useful instruments for promoting the general welfare, impersonally considered, or for any other higher-order reason. This argument is clearly set out in an essay on Sidgwick included in *The Sense of the Past* and in "The Primacy of Dispositions" and "The Structure of Hare's Theory" in *Philosophy as a Humanistic Discipline*.

Williams's objections seem to me more effective against utilitarianism than against theories of Kantian inspiration, which try to give independent weight to the personal perspective while pursuing a form of harmony among individual lives that can be universally acknowledged. It doesn't seem so difficult to value fidelity or loyalty for their own sake while at the same time recognizing that these values have to be included with others in a coherent system of standards that can apply to everyone. That is not mere dictation to the individual from the standpoint of the universe. And it combines naturally with a historical sense of the gradual expansion of the moral community, which can be expected to continue.

Three essays in *Philosophy as a Humanistic Discipline* are especially note-worthy. "Moral Responsibility and Political Freedom" is only seven pages long, but it applies Williams's characteristic resistance to excessive justification to the problem of punishment. (It should be read together with the discussion of blame in "Nietzsche's Minimalist Moral Psychology," in *The Sense of the Past*.) Williams argues that the concept of moral responsibility has a use in dealing with our response to offenses, but that it should not be taken too seri-ously and should not be turned into something metaphysically profound. He also says, strikingly, that retributive punishment is impossible in modern soci-ety, because "the paradigm of retributive punishment is a lynching, under the condition that the right person is being hanged.... Under modern demands on what counts as being sure of meeting that and other conditions, even an execution, if executions are allowed at all, is not going to reach the expressive standard of a lynching."

"The Human Prejudice" is a major essay, analyzing and defending our spe-cial concern for our fellow humans. Williams wonders mischievously whether Peter Singer, a leading critic of such "speciesism," feels uncomfortable about his position as a professor at Princeton University's Center for Human Values: "I should have thought it would have sounded to him rather like a Center for Aryan Values." Williams's main point is that being partial to humanity does not require a belief in the absolute importance of human beings. There is no cosmic point of view, and therefore no test of cosmic significance that we can either pass or fail. Those who criticize the privileged position of human beings in our ethical thought are confused:

> They suppose that we are in effect saying, when we exercise these
> distinctions between human beings and other creatures, that human

beings are more important, period, than those other creatures. That objection is simply a mistake.... These actions and attitudes need express no more than the fact that human beings are more important *to us*, a fact which is hardly surprising.

So humanism is just a form of group loyalty. Williams doesn't suggest that this warrants our brutality toward other species or complete indifference to their suffering, but he thinks our partiality to those who share our form of life does not need justification. He illustrates this with a wonderful science fiction fantasy of superior but disgusting visitors from outer space. And he concludes:

When the hope is to improve humanity to the point at which every aspect of its hold on the world can be justified before a higher court, the result is likely to be either self-deception, if you think you have succeeded, or self-hatred and self-contempt when you recognize that you will always fail. The self-hatred, in this case, is a hatred of humanity. Personally I think that there are many things to loathe about human beings, but their sense of their ethical identity as a species is not one of them.

Finally, the title essay, "Philosophy as a Humanistic Discipline," is a superb answer to the scientism that infects so much of contemporary philosophy. In his book on Descartes, Williams offered an illuminating interpretation of the aim of scientific objectivity as what he called the "absolute conception of reality." Here he asks:

Why should the idea that science and only science describes the world as it is in itself, independent of perspective, mean that there is no independent philosophical enterprise? That would follow only on the assumption that if there is an independent philosophical enterprise, its aim is to describe the world as it is in itself, independent of perspective. And why should we accept that?

It is a scientistic error to think that the concepts of physical science, because they are "potentially universal in their uptake and usefulness ... are somehow intrinsically superior to more local conceptions which are humanly and perhaps historically grounded."

The marks of philosophy are reflection and heightened self-awareness, not maximal transcendence of the human perspective. Reflection can deepen understanding without leaving that perspective. For that reason Williams values historical self-consciousness and deplores its neglect, or outright avoidance, by most analytic philosophers:

The reflective understanding of our ideas and motivations, which I take to be by general agreement a philosophical aim, is going to involve historical understanding.... Philosophy has to learn the lesson that conceptual description (or, more specifically, analysis) is not self-sufficient; and that such projects as deriving our concepts *a priori* from universal conditions of human life, though they indeed have a place (a greater place in some areas of philosophy than others), are likely to leave unexplained many features that provoke philosophical enquiry.

Williams applied these principles in the last book he published before his death, *Truth and Truthfulness: An Essay in Genealogy* (2002). With the essays in these three volumes, spanning his career, we have an indispensable summation of the complex thought of one of the finest minds of our age.

13

Wiggins on Human Solidarity

In *Ethics*[1] David Wiggins sets out to describe morality as a human phenomenon in a way that avoids the unreality he finds in most contemporary ethical theory. "What a fully grown-up moral philosophy might attempt," he says,

> is an account of morality that embraces the full gamut of
> moral predications, seeing them as mutually irreducible and
> mutually indispensable, allowing no primacy to character
> traits *or* virtues *or* practices *or* acts *or* states of affairs—or
> allowing primacy to all at once. Such a philosophy being
> neither consequentialist nor virtue-centred, might take on
> some of the subtlety of the moral phenomena themselves
> and of our moral deliverances upon them.

Wiggins resists without difficulty the common philosophical urge to seek understanding in simplicity and generality, and to unify morality under a single governing principle or value. He is especially opposed to consequentialist theories, which hold that the only things that matter for morality, ultimately, are better and worse overall outcomes, and to utilitarianism, the form of consequentialism that says the only outcomes that matter are pleasure and pain, or happiness and unhappiness.

---

1. David Wiggins, *Ethics: Twelve Lectures on the Philosophy of Morality* (Cambridge, Mass.: Harvard University Press, 2006).

Instead, Wiggins finds a number of distinct concerns and dispositions, each of which forms a part of our solidarity with our fellow human beings: the sense that certain acts are strictly forbidden, or unspeakable; the priority of fundamental needs; the idea of what is humanly livable; the weak but very general sentiment of benevolence; the values of honesty, fairness, and so forth. This does not result in a comprehensive system that tells us what we ought to do in every situation. But it expresses Wiggins's distinctive moral and political outlook, truculently antimodern but thoroughly humane, and committed to the application in moral thought of the idea of objective truth.

Ethics is framed as a series of lectures that start by introducing the audience to some leading moral philosophers—Plato, Aristotle, Hume, Kant, Mill, Hare, and others—through their responses to three questions: (a) What is the substance or content of morality? (b) What are the reasons to participate and persevere in morality? (c) What is the logical status of moral judgments, with respect to truth, objectivity, relativity, and the like? These questions, and their complex interdependence, are then gradually taken up and treated by Wiggins in themselves. His own position is closest to the naturalism of Hume, which he interprets however in a distinctive way, making it (in fact if not in name) a conception of practical reason with an Aristotelian flavor, whose reasons come from within ethics rather than from some higher or metaphysical standard of reasonableness. One of the achievements of the book is to displace Hume from his traditional role as the archenemy of reason in ethical theory.

In Wiggins's conception, an important feature of morality is its modesty. Its claims have to be humanly sustainable, and firmly grounded in dispositions that can readily become second nature to us. So Wiggins approves of Hume's invocation of the moderate motive of benevolence toward others, rather than the much more demanding impartial altruism that would be required to motivate "act-utilitarianism" (the view that you ought always to act in such a way as to maximize the sum total of everyone's happiness). And he rejects the Kantian objection that to ground morality in something as contingent as Humean fellow-feeling is inconsistent with the unconditional character of moral requirements:

> For us at least, for human beings I mean, this is not a contingency
> like just any old other contingency. Could we seriously undertake to
> change ourselves in order to remove our own (Humean) humanity?
> Or in order to remove our simply workaday reasonableness...?
> Without these, should we even recognize ourselves?

Wiggins also rejects the demand, posed by Glaucon and Adeimantus to Socrates in the *Republic*, to show that the motive for justice is so powerful that it will prevail even if the just man is tortured and reviled and the unjust is admired and rewarded. Moral motives should not have to pass this test; most of morality is nonheroic:

> The heroism of the Platonically just man is indeed a very special case of purity and strength of motive. But why assume that the relative weakness of the moral motive in the non-heroic cases taints the purity of this motive?...Why should one suppose that motives are tainted because, when the acts that they prompt one to do are followed by horrible punishment, the motives themselves grow weaker and weaker or more and more inert? Before they were driven out, were these not motives to kind or considerate action for the sake of the recipient or motives to honest dealing simply for honesty's own sake?

A different modesty manifests itself in the insistence that the main value in determining distributive justice is not equality but need. Wiggins has written about the moral and political importance of needs before, and about their nonrelative status. Ensuring that people have the means to provide for their most basic needs of survival and sustenance—that they should have enough—is part of human solidarity. But provision of what is valuable above that level should not be governed either by equality or by the imperative of maximizing total value, according to some comprehensive measure. There are many different values, rooted in the different possibilities of human life, all of which provide reasons, but they usually cannot be combined through a single principle to determine the one right thing to do. That way lies cost-benefit analysis and the abolition of Classics departments.

Morality's modesty is displayed in a particularly interesting way by Wiggins's contention that some situations are so extreme that they leave morality behind:

> When someone, an ordinary person who is not necessarily a consequentialist, points to some emergency so great that a beneficent agent will have to do something simply terrible in order to avert a disaster of almost unthinkable proportions, is the person who offers this advice really in the business of telling the beneficent person what it is *right* for him to do? Surely not....He is trying to show the beneficent person that that awful act is what he *has* to do, not what he "morally ought" to do. This is a new discipline and a new dialectic, lying altogether outside the remit of "deontology" as that was traditionally conceived...questions of right and wrong, of obligation,

or of acts the doing of which would be morally praiseworthy because they were done from a sense of duty... all these things will long since have gone out of the window. Their place will have been taken by dire (alleged) necessity.

Wiggins illustrates this with an example, from *The Cruel Sea* by Nicholas Monsarrat, of a captain who explodes a depth charge to destroy a submarine, knowing it will kill all the men swimming in the water who have escaped a cargo ship that has just been sunk. Wiggins adds, credibly, that such cases also cannot be understood by reference to a general moral requirement that we always act to produce the best outcome possible. If he is right, the common philosophical practice of using such extreme cases to test general moral theories is unjustified. They may not provide "moral data," in the usual sense, at all.

Yet morality pervades ordinary life, and the fact that it runs up against limits and does not form a single, all-encompassing system, in Wiggins's view, does not mean that it is not a domain of truth and falsehood, or that there are no moral facts. Morality is not just a set of propositions, but sometimes moral judgments can be expressed as propositions, and they can be true or false.

In explaining his cognitivist position, Wiggins makes effective use of the idea of there being "nothing else to think"—an idea he has used elsewhere. One cannot establish moral truths from outside morality any more than one can establish mathematical truths from outside mathematics. But the sign that we are in each case dealing with judgments that are objectively true or false is that often the best explanation of someone's coming to believe that $7 + 5 = 12$, or that slavery is wrong, is one that leaves the explainer himself no room to deny that these things are true. Once we have set out in full a contemporary European's moral reasons for thinking slavery is wrong, there is nothing else to think but that it is wrong. We are left without a foothold for doubt, either about whether the judgment has a truth value at all, or whether it is true rather than false. I believe that one cannot ask for more than this in a defense of truth and objectivity for a domain of discourse.

Wiggins insists that the objectivity of morality is not undermined by the fact that the source of these judgments is in a sense subjective, since it lies in the dispositions and responses of human morality, and not in some independent structure of the universe. "Objective," he argues, is not the opposite of "subjective," and "slavery is wrong" is an example of an objective truth that is also subjective. He points out that in this objectivism he departs from Hume. But Wiggins adds: "The human scale of values is timeless or (if you prefer) it reaches backwards and forwards *to all times*. The fact that *its recognition* has the history it has need not deter Hume from thinking ingratitude as hateful or despicable in itself." The explanation of a judgment that *p* that leaves one with nothing else to think but *p* Wiggins calls a "vindicatory explanation," and he believes Hume's style of moral analysis is designed to provide vindicatory explanations. Hume, he says, "is a genealogist who is, in addition, *committed* to that which he explains—prepared that is, when enough of the pieces are falling into place, to try to vindicate most (but certainly not all) of the attitudes and convictions he seeks to explain."

Wiggins is profoundly conservative—the only person I know who treats "agenda" as a plural in English as it is in Latin. He detests the overrationalized public ethic of perpetual transformative improvement—the dispossession of indigenous or nomadic peoples in the name of economic development, or the debasement of higher education in the name of efficiency and equal opportunity. Intellectually, these evils are represented and politically supported by utilitarianism, and the consequentialism that gives it its structure. Consequentialism means that all choice, and the justification of all moral principles, must depend on the way we assign value to outcomes, and the way we add up those values. It means anything can be weighed against anything else.

Wiggins's central objection is that much of morality, like much of life, is not based on the maximization of value in this sense. The wrongness of murder, or of betrayal, does not lie in its disvalue. The idea of what is wrong, forbidden, unspeakable, is the idea of what is in itself morally impossible to do, what in itself is counter to human life and its purposes. If it is replaced by a quantifiable value, "there will be nothing so terrible that an agent cannot be required to do that very thing in order to dissuade/prevent others from doing more of it, on a grander scale, with yet more dreadful outcome." Someone who tries to reduce everything to value and disvalue in this way misunderstands ethical language and the attitude toward our fellow human beings that it expresses.

The basis of the ethical, according to Wiggins, is solidarity, which shows itself in a "primitive aversion from acts that appear as a direct assault by one personal being upon another, acts such as murder, wounding, injury, plunder, pillage, the harming of innocents, the repaying of good with gratuitous evil, false witness." Given this foundation, more positive social virtues of cooperation can develop, and morality can extend to the conventions of property and contract, and to the promotion of further positive values. But the basic condition of solidarity must retain its priority.

Wiggins extends the view into politics with a discussion of justice that resists the primarily institutional focus of most modern theories, in favor of a conception by which the justice of a society is inseparable from the justice of its individual members. Though he finds this neo-Aristotelian view in the writings of Bertrand de Jouvenel, Wiggins notes that it has something in common with G. A. Cohen's criticism of Rawls's restriction of his principles of justice to the institutional structure of society—but without Cohen's egalitarianism.

A consequentialist will admit that solidarity is certainly better than selfishness, but that to evaluate moral dispositions we still need to occupy a more rational and impersonal standpoint. We can keep those dispositions that produce good outcomes, while those that do not can be changed gradually through moral formation and education. Why should that not count as moral progress? Wiggins, however, regards such regimentation as an abuse of the idea of practical reason. Ethical thought must take moral dispositions seriously in themselves, and will lose its sense if it tries to transcend them, modeling itself on a scientific form of rationality. The desirability of producing better overall outcomes simply lacks the rational authority to overrule the reasons coming from more basic moral dispositions.

By contrast, a Kantian evaluation of principles of conduct that maintains a separate concern for each individual is probably more in keeping with the primitive solidarity on which Wiggins believes morality depends—even though Wiggins definitely prefers the human solidarity of Hume to the rational solidarity of Kant. Wiggins is always a complex writer, and this cannot really be regarded as an introductory work, but it is a rich and eloquent book, whose moral sanity is hard to resist.

14

O'Shaughnessy on the Stream of Consciousness

Philosophy, unlike most other subjects, does not try to extend our knowledge by discovering new information about the world. It tries to deepen our understanding by reflection on what is already closest to us—the experiences, thoughts, concepts, and activities that make up our lives, and that ordinarily escape notice because they are so familiar. Philosophy begins by finding utterly mysterious the things that pervade our everyday lives, such as language, perception, value, and truth. For everyday purposes we don't have to know how these things are possible: We talk, we see what is in front of us, and we judge that this action is wrong or that assertion true. But it is possible, in the tradition deriving from Plato, to stop and think about what we are really doing, not for a practical purpose but just in order to understand what lies beneath the familiar surface of life.

Human consciousness, which is at the core of everything we do and think, is one of the principal targets of such philosophical understanding. In our time the advance of physical and biological science makes possible the search for some of its physiological conditions, but there is a more basic understanding of consciousness that remains a philosophical task, and that is surprisingly undeveloped—an understanding that we can pursue only from within. It has occupied phenomenologists like Husserl and Sartre, and empiricists like Hume and Russell. Even if empirical science starts from the evidence provided by conscious experience, understanding the nature of that starting point is still mainly the concern of philosophers.

Brian O'Shaughnessy's philosophical career has been occupied with our most basic relations to the world. Some years ago he published an enormous book called *The Will*,[1] about how we connect to the world in the outward direction, when we act. Now he has published another enormous book that goes in the other direction. In *Consciousness and the World*,[2] O'Shaughnessy examines the world's impact on us through perception—though he emphasizes that we are anything but passive when we perceive the world around us; that, too, involves the will.

O'Shaughnessy's approach to perceptual consciousness is distinctive in being simultaneously physical and phenomenological. He takes us and other animals to be physical beings—parts of the physical world—each of which has a perspective on that world and an inner life of some kind. An inquiry into conscious experience cannot be based merely on the observation of external behavior, but it also cannot be carried out in abstraction from our physical nature. The understanding of the inner life of the person who is conscious must include the physical body from the start. In his new book, O'Shaughnessy develops an account of human consciousness as a continual process by which we come to know about the vast physical world around us through awareness of what is going on in a small part of it, namely, our own body.

It could hardly be otherwise, since all information about the rest of the world reaches us through our bodies. But when I gaze out my window toward the Hudson River and watch the planes coming down to land at Newark airport, and see the stars emerge in the sky as night falls, the complexity and radical indirectness of the process is completely hidden from me. I seem just to see these things directly, and of course I do not. A full account of what actually happens would be extremely intricate, and we have only part of it. Since Plato and Aristotle began to worry about the question, a great deal has been learned about what takes place between the stars and the retina, and much is currently being learned about the physical effects of retinal stimuli on the brain, but what goes on in the mind remains very difficult to describe, even though it is in a sense closer to us than anything else could be.

To his credit O'Shaughnessy, unlike most contemporary philosophers, uses the term "consciousness" in its correct English sense, to mean a state of awareness of the world around us—roughly, the state of being awake. For some reason the term is commonly used more broadly in philosophical discourse to refer to any psychological state that has a subjective, experienced character.

---

1. Brian O'Shaughnessy, *The Will: A Dual Aspect Theory* (Cambridge: Cambridge University Press, 1980; second edition, 2008).

2. Brian O'Shaughnessy, *Consciousness and the World* (Oxford: Oxford University Press, 2000).

For this latter category, O'Shaughnessy uses the term "experience," which is more accurate. Dreams, for example, are experiences we have when we are not conscious. (Other psychological states, like knowing, believing, and intending, need not be immediately experienced to exist, nor are they usually present in consciousness, though they can have large conscious effects, as when my long-standing familiarity with the Beatles causes me instantly to recognize the melody of "Yesterday.")

The stream of consciousness is what we all live in. That expression is now associated with a literary form in which a character's inner monologue of thoughts and associations is presented accurately and is very different from the orderly outward forms of his life in the world. But the true stream of consciousness is far richer and far less verbal than anything described in *Ulysses*. Think about what happens to you during any two minutes spent walking on a city street—the flood of sensations, perceptions, and feelings that courses through you, most of them hardly drawing your attention. The multiplicity and density of detail is far greater than even the richest collection of verbalized thoughts or conversations with yourself that may have been going on at the same time. The process by which the world impinges on us at all times and the constantly shifting apprehension of our relation to it are too enormous for us to fully grasp.

O'Shaughnessy wants to analyze this process insofar as it is accessible to the heightened self-consciousness of philosophical reflection. Consciousness as he conceives it is filled with experience, but experience of a special kind. Unlike the experience in dreams or imaginings, the experience of consciousness is subject to a ceaseless rational control that tries to make sense of the surrounding world and our place in it: It is shaped by the requirement of reality—of placing ourselves as physical beings in a physically real world. It is necessarily aimed at the truth.

Even when its contents do not change, consciousness is never static but always proceeding in time, so that it apprehends both change and changelessness. Whether you are crossing a street, reading a letter, making a phone call, or merely staring at the ceiling, your experience includes at every point the sense of what is immediately past and the readiness for what may come next; consciousness prepares us to act in the light of what is happening and about to happen. It gives us our only acquaintance with time and, through changes in the relation between ourselves and other things over time, our knowledge of space as well, by tracking our movements and the change in how things look and feel as we move around them. In all this, our unformulated sense of the location, posture, and boundaries of our own body plays an essential part. The accomplishments of an ordinary pedestrian are technically as amazing as those of Fred Astaire.

Most of O'Shaughnessy's book is about perception, especially visual perception. He presents a theory that is rather old-fashioned and these days rarely defended: the theory that all our perception of the outer world depends on awareness of psychological items in our own minds called sense-data. We don't think of perception in this way, he argues, but that is what is really going on. We never "just see" any physical object: To see it, we must see the light reflected from it that strikes our retinas. And to see that light we must become aware of the visual sensations, as he calls them—describable in terms of color and shape—that are directly caused by the chemical effects of the light on the retina and their effects on the optic nerve and the brain. (O'Shaughnessy's view is consistent with the hypothesis that visual sensations are in some sense identical with certain physical effects in the brain, but this aspect of the mind-body problem is not his subject.)

The full set of your visual sensations at any time comprises your "visual field." O'Shaughnessy maintains that you can be visually aware of these psychological items, as you can be visually aware of an afterimage, which exists only in your mind and cannot be seen by other people; even if they looked into your brain, they would see only the physical features of the brain event that corresponds to it. If the chain of causal links is sufficiently reliable, we get what he calls the Transitivity of Attention: "Presence in the visual field of a round orange sensation *is* presence in the visual field of a cylindrical beam of orange light, which *is* in turn presence therein of an orange sphere. . . . [The attention] has merely to make any one of these three listed items its object, to make the other two simultaneously its object." Perception of the orange is not, in other words, accomplished by inference (I need not believe that it is an orange in order to see it). It is guaranteed by the strict causal link from object, to light, to nerves, to sensation. It is that causal link that makes it possible for a single event to be all these things at once: the awareness of a visual sensation, the seeing of light, the seeing of the near surface of an object, and the seeing of the object.

Without sensation we would not see, but it is another important feature of O'Shaughnessy's view that there is vastly more in the visual field, and in our other sensory data, than reaches our attention—and that even when we are not aware of these sensations, they exist. The attention has a severely limited capacity at any moment, and it must select first of all from the plethora of content in our own minds.

What kind of existence do unnoticed sensations have? The question is a new version, transferred to the interior of the mind, of the old philosophical chestnut, whether a tree falling unheard in the forest makes a sound. What about the ticking of the clock when you don't notice it? The question is not whether the clock ticks, but whether it produces an auditory sensation in you whether you notice it or not. O'Shaughnessy uses the example of tinnitus, a condition with which I am familiar: In my case, the symptom takes the form of a constant, faint hissing noise that no one else can hear. Most of the time I don't notice it, but I only have to listen for it and it is there, at any time of day or night. Obviously its physical cause, whatever that may be, is present whether I hear it or not (like the sound waves in the forest), but is the sensation itself present even when I don't notice it? O'Shaughnessy says yes, and that the same can be said for a large part of what makes up your visual field or your tactile sensations at any moment. If you now direct your attention to the pressure of your left shoe on your heel, you will become suddenly aware in experience of a sensation that was already there, unnoticed and—paradoxical though it sounds—unexperienced.

So O'Shaughnessy has introduced a threefold distinction among phenomena to which many people have indiscriminately applied the term "consciousness": sensations (which need not be experienced), experience (which need not be conscious), and consciousness. In the case of vision, he believes the selectivity of awareness with respect to sensation is extreme, because of the richness of the sense data. When you see a field of daffodils, each daffodil registers its contribution to your visual field through direct action on the retina, but you can't possibly attend to all of them. What your attention grasps is the whole field, and that is the content of your conscious experience, even though images of the particular daffodils are present in the visual field and you could become aware of them if you attended to them individually. But until you do that, the images of particular flowers are "a noticeable and unnoticed part of the noticed."

The selectivity and limited capacity of attention is a pervasive fact of life. But do these auditory, visual, and tactile sensations that fall outside the scope of our limited attention at any time have real psychological existence, as O'Shaughnessy claims? Or does their existence consist merely in the possibility of their being noticed? And how much can philosophical reflection do to answer the question? Introspection won't settle it, since what you notice when you attend to a sensation doesn't tell you what happens when you don't attend to it. Does attention have the effect of making sensations spring into existence that weren't there until you looked or listened for them? When I shift my attention to listen to the ticking of the clock or the conversation at the next table in a restaurant, or to my private hissing noise, the inner sounds certainly seem to be there, waiting for me to hear them, but though O'Shaughnessy explores the two hypotheses at length, and I am inclined to agree with his judgment, I think the question remains open.

O'Shaughnessy wants to "prise apart two closely intertwined psychological items: the visual field, and our awareness of it. The independent psychological reality of the visual field *is* the existence of visual sensations or visual sense-data"—sensations of which we are often not aware. What is the importance of this issue? It is that O'Shaughnessy wants to resist the overintellectualization of the mind. He wants to establish that the higher mental functions rest on a brute foundation that is meaningless, uninterpreted, and directly linked to the physical body and the direct impact on the body of the rest of the physical world. (In his earlier book on the will, he argued persuasively for a similar basis of action that was below the level of conscious intention.) The first stage in perception is the direct physical causation of a wealth of sensations, imprinting the world in our mental flesh, so to speak. Only when the attention focuses on and makes sense of some of this material does experience arise—experience that can be the subject of introspection. And then, from experience, beliefs and knowledge can arise, along with the awareness of the world that makes intentional action possible.

This view goes against the widespread current tendency to see all psychological states as pervaded with thought, belief, concepts, and intentions—with meaning of some kind. According to that approach, the sensory qualities of a visual impression are simply identified with its representation of the external properties of objects we perceive—the roundness and orangeness of the image, for example, are identified by many philosophers with its seeming to me that there is an orange, or something very like an orange, in front of me. (This view is called representationism.) O'Shaughnessy objects, first, that I can only notice the orange by noticing the orange disk in my visual field and, second, that the sensory orange disk may be there without my noticing it. If my eyes happen to be resting on a fruit bowl while a political catastrophe is announced on the radio, the orange disk will be included in my visual field, but I may not notice either it or the orange.

For O'Shaughnessy, then, the attention puts together the stream of consciousness from a selected portion of the abundant raw material of sensation, and it shapes that material into experiences and knowledge of the world, to be used in determining at every moment what to expect and what to do next. This is a compelling picture and seems true to experience. On reflection, it is hard to deny that the contents of our minds are much larger than our fully conscious selves. The attentive self that is the subject of consciousness is in some sense the inhabitant and explorer of a vast mental territory, and uninterpreted data in our minds form the first boundary between the conscious self and the external world.

What is needed to complete this picture is an understanding of what attention itself is. It can't be depicted as an internal perceiver of the contents of the mind without leading to a regress—since in that case the original sense data would have to cause further sense data of which the attention became aware, and the same question would arise about how it notices them. O'Shaughnessy's account is not easy to understand. He says that the awareness of an experience simply is the experience itself. But what happens when an unnoticed sensation becomes part of conscious experience by being noticed? O'Shaughnessy says it becomes immediately available for use in rational action and belief, having been picked out by the attention in its constant effort to make sense of the world. The attention, for him, is really a mental manifestation of the will, and consciousness is the product of the constant activity of the mental rational will in maintaining an intelligible and usable version of the world and our place in it.

While this may be a good account of the function of consciousness, it isn't an account of the intrinsic difference between a noticed and an unnoticed sensation. But perhaps there is nothing more to be said about this, and we must be content with O'Shaughnessy's aim of describing how the attention shapes the experiences of the present moment into an intelligible system.

Anyone who has experienced insomnia knows that the essence of consciousness is mental activity, and that we cannot lose consciousness unless we manage to give it up and become passive vehicles of sensation and fantasy, no longer imposing order or sense on them. O'Shaughnessy has some very interesting and astute discussions of dreams, drunkenness, and hallucinations—states in which the rational control of experience characteristic of full consciousness is severely diminished or absent, the exercise of will is weakened, and the connection to reality is broken.

He also presents a related theory of the imagination. He holds that imagination is very different from perception, in that it does not contain any "unnoticed but noticeable" parts. (This was also observed by Sartre.[3]) If I imagine a bed of daffodils, there need be no specific number of daffodils that I imagine; but when I actually see a bed of daffodils, then whether I notice them individually or not, there is a specific number of daffodils that I see and a specific number of daffodil images in my visual field. This difference reflects the absence from the imagination of the direct causal control of my senses by the external world that occurs in perception. The content of imagination, O'Shaughnessy argues, is fully determined by what is imagined—here, for example, a bed of daffodils, with no number specified. It is not merely a pale form of perceptual image.

---

3. Jean-Paul Sartre, *L'Imaginaire: Psychologie Phénoménologique de l'Imagination* (Paris: Gallimard, 1940).

I don't know whether this interesting claim is true, and I doubt that its truth or falsity can be determined by philosophical reflection alone. I have a similar uncertainty about O'Shaughnessy's sense-datum theory and his argument for the autonomy of the visual field. Certainly these are credible positions, and they are carefully developed. But I believe that physiological evidence would also be relevant to a final judgment about the interaction between attention, sensation, and sensory input.

O'Shaughnessy's only excursion into physiological psychology is a long discussion of the pathological condition called blindsight, in which the brain-damaged subject has no visual experience but can still, in certain circumstances, make accurate guesses as to what is before his eyes. Even though he may consider himself blind, the remaining parts of his visual system can still have a direct influence on his beliefs. O'Shaughnessy is mainly concerned to argue that this response is not "seeing," because it does not include visual experience. But there are also facts about the normal operation of vision that complicate the picture.

Consider, for example, the operation of a component of the neurological apparatus of vision called the dorsal system.[4] The dorsal system allows visual input to play a part in the control of action without going through consciousness. When you run on a beach, for example, you avoid stepping on stones in your path, not because you perceive them but before you perceive them, in virtue of a direct contribution of visual information to the control of action. In other words, your eyes can guide your feet without giving you a visual experience first.

This is known from the different effects of injuries to different pathways by which information from the retina reaches the brain. Because it involves the subtle control of intentional action, it is different from the more familiar fact that one reflexively withdraws one's hand from a hot surface before feeling the pain. These phenomena seem to show that the data of vision, insofar as they are directly caused by neural input, are more complex than can be captured in the idea of a single visual field whose contents are all sensations, whether noticed or not. Some of the inputs that are not noticed may be present in other forms than as sensations.

Another relevant example is provided by the evidence that the visual field cannot be described simply as an expanse with the color specified at each point, like the pixels on a computer screen. O'Shaughnessy argues that this bare minimum "atomistic" account is the one that describes the "visual given," namely,

---

4. See A. David Milner and Melvyn A. Goodale, *The Visual Brain in Action* (Oxford: Oxford University Press, 1995).

what is there before the attention goes to work on it. But much more process-
ing seems to go on even at the earliest stages of the physical production of
visual sensation, including, for example, detecting the boundaries of objects,
identifying them as distinct things, and tracking their movements. Such pro-
cessed visual data may already be part of the physically caused "raw material"
on which the attention operates to generate conscious experience. Well-known
studies of specialized detectors in the visual cortex point to such a conclusion.[5]
They may not prove the conclusion; rival theories have to be weighed against all
the evidence. But if we take seriously the conception of the senses as paths by
which the physical world directly affects the mind, physiological evidence for
the antecedent receptive structure of the mind becomes important.

O'Shaughnessy is a remarkably gifted and solitary philosopher who pays
almost no attention to anyone else, and it would be naïve to expect him to
behave like an ordinary member of the profession. Still, to read his book is a
Stakhanovite task, even for someone who has spent a lifetime studying philosophy. It has seven hundred closely printed pages of dense argument, with
hardly any references to the vast literature on these topics, and a Proustian
exhaustiveness of detail that suggests, no doubt wrongly, that we are getting
the entire contents of the author's mind. My description gives only the bare
bones of the theory; it would be impossible to convey the flavor of the book
without quoting, for example, the detailed discussion of the forms of temporal
knowledge someone can possess while in a coma, or the explanation of why the
visual detectability of a particle passing through a cloud chamber doesn't mean
that the particle is visible. I fear that the sheer volume of O'Shaughnessy's work
will deter all but the most dedicated readers, and I get the uneasy feeling that
O'Shaughnessy doesn't care. This is too bad, because the book offers a great
deal of insight about the most conspicuous and least understood thing in the
universe—ourselves.

If we are to make progress over the long term in understanding how the
mind fits into the world, it will take detailed phenomenological investigations
like O'Shaughnessy's as well as research on the brain and on behavior. There
is a danger of assuming that we all know what we're talking about when we
set out to investigate visual perception and other forms of consciousness scientifically: It may seem that the subjective phenomena are familiar and we
must search for their hidden physical basis, as we might investigate the structure of the eye. But that is too simple. The phenomena to be explained are in
this case much more complex than our intuitive grasp of them reveals, and to
deepen our understanding of them is in part a philosophical task, which must

5. See David Hubel, *Eye, Brain, and Vision* (New York: W. H. Freeman, 1988).

be carried out if the scientific questions are to be posed correctly. To seek inner understanding of the kind pursued by O'Shaughnessy, not by abstracting the perspective of consciousness from the physical world but by recognizing the primitive embeddedness of consciousness in that world, seems to me the right path to follow. This is so even if a great deal will remain hidden from a priori reflection, and equal attention will have to be paid to the physical evidence.

15

Sartre: The Look and the Problem of Other Minds

Sartre's discussion of the existence of Others in *Being and Nothingness*[1] is a distinctive and original part of his philosophy, which ramifies in his remarks on the body and sexuality. But I want to examine it as a contribution to the understanding of the traditional problem of other minds, and the broader problem of which that is one expression—the problem of how we can understand our own mind, our own subjectivity, as one instance of a type of being of which there are many examples, all contained somehow in a common world that has an objective existence.

The problem of other minds is often introduced as an epistemological problem: How do we know that the human and other living animal organisms we can observe in the world around us have any inner subjective experiences at all? All we can really observe is the outsides and insides of their bodies—their behavior and physiology—so that belief in their minds seems to be based on an inference from these observations to something else that we cannot observe: a subjective experiential and intentional life that to some degree resembles our own.

Much has been said about this inference. It does not seem very strong if interpreted as a case of simple enumerative induction, since

1. Jean-Paul Sartre, *l'Etre et le Néant* (Paris: Gallimard, 1943); translated by Hazel E. Barnes, *Being and Nothingness* (New York: Philosophical Library, 1956). All quotations are from part 3, chapter 1: "The Existence of Others."

it is based (for each person) on only one example of directly observed correlation between the mental and the physical. It seems much stronger if it is based on the general assumption of the uniformity of nature, since nature would be intolerably and inexplicably arbitrary if I were the only organism that possessed consciousness.

But this epistemological issue does not get at the really deep problem of other minds. In order to pose the epistemological question—How do I know that others have minds?—we have to already understand the proposition for which we are seeking evidence or confirmation. And that is what seems difficult, if we start out from our own case. For how can we so much as form the idea of a sensation that we do not feel, for example, on the basis of a sensation that we do feel? It is not enough, as Wittgenstein observed, simply to locate the sensation in another body—just as we cannot give sense to the idea that it is 5 o'clock on the sun by saying that it is the same time there as it is when it is 5 o'clock here.

This is the conceptual rather than the epistemological problem of solipsism: not, how can we be sure that other humans have minds? but how can it even mean anything to speak of a mind other than my own? Understanding the idea of "*the Other*, that is the self which *is not* myself" is, as Sartre insists, the fundamental problem. Given an understanding of that idea, I can pose and perhaps answer the epistemological problem and can conclude that it is highly probable that the human organisms around me are other selves. But such an argument from probability cannot solve the prior problem of showing that its conclusion is intelligible. That must somehow be given in advance.

Sartre's view is that if we try to construct the idea of the Other on the basis of our knowledge of ourselves, or on the basis of our knowledge of the rest of the world, we will not succeed. To put it in his terminology, if I start with being-for-itself, with which I am acquainted in my case through the Cartesian *cogito*, and being-in-itself, which I observe in the world of objects, there is no way, using those materials, to arrive at the idea of a for-itself that is other than myself. What is needed is an unmediated, ground floor presentation of the Other, no less immediate than my understanding of my own subjectivity.

We should not have to prove the existence of the Other any more than we have to prove our own. The *cogito*, says Sartre, is not a proof of my existence but a way of seeing that I have always known my own existence and cannot doubt it. What we need, says Sartre, is an equivalent of the *cogito* for the case of the Other:

> Actually I have always known that I existed, I have never ceased to
> practice the *cogito*. Similarly my resistance to solipsism—which is as

lively as any I should offer to an attempt to doubt the *cogito*—proves that I have always known that the Other existed, that I have always had a total though implicit comprehension of his existence, that this "pre-ontological" comprehension comprises a surer and deeper understanding of the nature of the Other and the relation of his being to my being than all the theories which have been built around it. If the Other's existence is not a vain conjecture, a pure fiction, this is because there is a sort of *cogito* concerning it.

Before taking up his account of this *cogito* of the Other, I want to contrast it with the method most commonly used in the analytic tradition to replace the move from myself to others in dealing with the problem of other minds. That method, which has taken various forms, is to resist the first-person starting point by insisting that the concept of mind is a public concept, applicable from the start not just to myself but rather to myself only as an instance of something of which there are other instances. More concretely, the first-person conception of my own mind that is the starting point for the *cogito* is said to be inextricable, in a way Descartes failed to understand, from the third-person conditions of application of mental concepts by myself to others and by others to myself—on the basis of observable behavior and other objective conditions.

If that is right, the problem of other minds cannot even be posed. The concept of my own mind is already that of an "other" mind, in the sense that its existence is given by objectively detectable criteria involving the body. The entire reductionist tradition in the philosophy of mind, from behaviorism through causal role theories to functionalism, takes this form. The same view also underlies the more sophisticated nonreductionist accounts of the insepa-rability of first-person and third-person application of mental concepts put forward by Wittgenstein and Strawson.[2]

Sartre's response to the problem is emphatically not reductionist. He does not propose to find subjectivity, his own or that of the Other, unproblematically present as part of the natural order that we can all observe around us. That would be to ignore the problem by interpreting the self as a special type of object—in fact, to construe it as an example of being-in-itself.

Sartre never considers an anti-Cartesian view like Wittgenstein's, which had not yet appeared when he wrote *Being and Nothingness*, but he certainly rejects behaviorism. He recognizes, unlike the reductionist tradition, that the relation of mind to the publicly observable natural order is deeply problematic,

---

2. In *Philosophical Investigations* and *Individuals*, respectively.

and that it is not at all transparent what is going on when I ascribe subjectivity to the person on the park bench opposite me. And as a corollary, he recognizes that the relation of my subjectivity to my own body, and to my existence as an object in the world, is likewise problematic. His response to the problem of other minds attempts to do justice to this strangeness, and not to abandon the authority of the *cogito*.

Sartre also rejects as insufficient Husserl's response to solipsism, namely, that the reality of others is presupposed by the inescapable idea of an objective world, whose contents can be perceived not only by myself. This is too indirect, more like a transcendental argument than an immediate and indubitable presentation of the Other as subject. It does not provide us with a grasp of the reality of a for-itself that is not myself.

What Sartre finds to occupy the position corresponding to the *cogito* for a demonstration of the Other is *the Look*—or rather the for-itself's awareness of the Look. This has the advantage of solving two philosophical problems at once: First, it provides an immediate and noninferential grasp of the Other, and second, it reveals me to myself as an object in the world, and not just a subject. The Look is the immediate experience of being perceived, and it gives me both the Other and my own objecthood all at once. In Sartre's terms, it reveals the Other not as an in-itself or as an analogue to the for-itself, but in the immediate being-for-others that is a further aspect of our consciousness and that is understood through an expanded use of the *cogito*.

The memorable scenario by which Sartre presents the Look includes the element of shame, one of the fundamental forms that apprehension of the Look can take. Sartre imagines himself, "moved by jealousy, curiosity, or vice," looking through a keyhole from an empty passageway into an occupied room. His consciousness is filled with the spectacle of what is going on behind the door. He is not reflectively aware of himself, but is simply engaged in unreflective consciousness of what he sees and hears. "But all of a sudden I hear footsteps in the hall. Someone is looking at me! What does this mean? It means that I am suddenly affected in my being and that essential modifications appear in my structure—modifications which I can apprehend and fix conceptually by means of the reflective *cogito*."

What happens is that I suddenly experience my self as something perceived by the Other, as someone peeking through a keyhole. This is the self not merely for itself, but for the Other, and the recognition that it is I whom the other sees in this demeaning posture is the experience of shame. But this would be impossible if the Other were merely an object in the world, however complex. In feeling shame, I have an immediate grasp of the fact that the world is not just my world, that in fact I am myself an object in the world of the Other:

"It is shame...which reveals to me the Other's look and myself at the end of that look. It is the shame...which makes me *live*, not *know* the situation of being looked at."

This, then, is the noninferential, nonprobabilistic direct grasp of the Other that constitutes an extension of the *cogito*. It is supposed to show that the recognition and understanding of the Other is inseparable from the structure of my own consciousness and therefore is as fundamental as Descartes' *cogito* shows my awareness of my own existence to be. The concept of the Other is directly given and not constructed by inference or analogy on the basis of my idea of myself. (Remember, we are talking here about the *idea* of the Other, not about the epistemological grounds for applying that idea to particular cases, once we have it. In fact, I may experience the Look, hence recognition of the reality of the Other and the falsity of solipsism, even if I have only imagined the footsteps in the hall.)

It is crucial that this is not an apprehension of the Other as object, but as a for-itself for which I am an object. The Look reveals me to myself as an object in the Other's world. If I turn the tables and see the Other as an object, I no longer experience myself as an object for him:

> In fact from the moment that the Other appears to me as an
> object, his subjectivity becomes a simple property of the object
> considered.... The-Other-as-Object "has" a subjectivity as this hollow
> box has "an inside." In this way I *recover* myself, for I can not be *an*
> *object for an object*. I certainly do not deny that the Other remains
> connected with me "inside him," but the consciousness which he
> has of me, since it is consciousness-as-an-object, appears to me as
> pure interiority without efficacy. It is just one property among others
> of that "inside," something comparable to a sensitized plate in the
> closed compartment of a camera.

Sartre has a great deal more to say in elaboration of the themes of interpersonal awareness, objecthood, the body, and many other topics that arise from this phenomenological starting point. It is clear that he has described an important phenomenon, and that its exploration is the source of rich and complex insights. But I will limit myself to asking whether he has succeeded in his initial aim—to find the answer to solipsism in an equivalent to the *cogito* for the reality of the Other.

If we set aside possible doubts about the legitimacy of a pure first-person starting point, there are two fairly obvious questions about Sartre's claim. First, why doesn't the experience of the Look depend on a logically prior grasp of the Other, rather than providing it without presuppositions? Second, the idea of other subjects has to extend far beyond the range of those humans for whom I can become an object in the way that can make me feel shame or even feel perceived, so how can the Look be what reveals the general rejection of solipsism?

But let me also set aside this second problem. The recognition of lower forms of consciousness may after all depend on an analogical inference, but that inference can get started only if I am already able to recognize immediately and noninferentially the full human form of a for-itself that is not me, and for whom I can be an object.

To return, then, to the first problem: When I hear, or think I hear, footsteps in the corridor I suddenly become aware of myself not as a subject but as an object in someone else's world—a peeping Tom. Sartre contends that this cannot be a compound built up out of the independent concept of the Other together with the belief that in this case a particular Other has caught me looking through a keyhole. It cannot be like that, because the full concept of the Other is not independently available. It is analogous to the case of the *cogito*. The *cogito* is not a compound built up out of the prior and independent concept of the I together with the idea of thought. Rather, the I is revealed only as the subject of this thought. Similarly, the concept of the Other is extracted from the more basic experience of shame, which is a form of the experience of being seen. Shame reveals the reality of the Other as subject, rather than presupposing it. When I hear the footsteps in the corridor, I have an immediate understanding that I am an object of contempt, and from this I grasp that there is or could be an Other for whom I am that object.

I think the logical reversal here embodies a real insight about the preintellectual place of other minds in the structure of individual consciousness. Sartre makes a compelling case that our basic conception of other minds is not arrived at by analogy, and that we find it instead in our primitive feelings—which on analysis reveal themselves as feelings of being-for-others. Perhaps shame and pride, Sartre's examples, are a bit sophisticated, and more attention should be given to forms of the Look that even infants can experience, the Look that makes me feel loved or threatened, but in any case an object for an Other, who is not merely an object in my world. At a certain point the infant experiences the world looking back at him. Without this primitive sense of being-for-others in the for-itself's feelings about itself, the much more epistemically sophisticated inferential knowledge of others on the basis of behavioral and other observations could not on its own deliver to us the full reality of other minds. It is evident that first-person and third-person mental concepts are also logically interdependent in other ways, but I believe Sartre has shown that the Look is an essential aspect of the link between them.

Index